The Homosexual Challenge

A Christian Response to an Age of Sexual Politics

by Donald L. Faris

FT
PUBLICATIONS

Faith Today Publications is the publishing division of the Evangelical Fellowship of Canada.

Printed and bound in Canada by Hignell Printing Limited

Canadian Cataloguing in Publication Data

Faris, Donald L.
The homosexual challenge: a Christian response to an age of sexual politics

Previously published under title: Trojan Horse.
Includes bibliographical references.
ISBN 0-9695596-2-3

I. Homosexuality – Religious aspects – Christianity.
I. Title. II. Title: Trojan horse.

BR115.H6F3 1993 261.8'35766 C93-094757-6

Faith Today Publications
#1, 175 Riviera Drive
Markham, Ontario, Canada
L3R 5J6

Contents

To my wife Margaret
and my sons, Paul
and Mark.

Introduction

Anyone who thinks that the current controversy in the Christian churches about homosexual practice is *only* about homosexual practice is greatly mistaken. The central issue is whether the revelation of the Scriptures about the nature and purpose of humanity is still valid today – or whether we should be looking for another revelation?

The idea that homosexual practices (that is, sexual activities with members of one's own gender) are "just as good as" marriage between men and women is only part of a wider sexual belief system grounded in the individualism that is the dominant religion of the liberal middle class in North America. "If it feels good to me and it does no harm (according to my personal definition of harm), it must be okay" is the basic creed espoused by most members of the North American middle class today. And a homosexual lifestyle seems okay to many such people.

Many Christians are torn by questions surrounding these issues. For example, perhaps friends or popular clergy are homosexual. They ask me, are you trying to say that homosexuals are not nice people? Our society is increasingly liberal regarding homosexual practice. Is it then "homophobic" and unloving to oppose these practices, as some claim? During recent decades, many ministers have preached the social gospel and liberation theology. Must a gospel of liberation now support homosexual practice? Let's look at these three questions before starting on the following chapters, where they will be dealt with in more depth.

1. Aren't homosexuals nice people?

Well, some are, some are not. I know people who are homosexuals and people who are heterosexuals; I also know alcoholics and total abstainers, as well as Conservatives and Communists. Some are nice people. Some are not. What has this to do with the truth or falsehood of their assertions? And what does it have to do with the morality of their behaviour?

Let me clarify the issue: Some people cannot think clearly about any issue because their world is divided simply into people who are "nice" and people who are "not nice." For example, they are uncertain where they stand on the issue of homosexual practice among Christians because they claim to know a practising homosexual who is a "nice person". Well, so do I. I also know practising adulterers who are "nice people". But, for example, if a man's friends think that he is basically a "nice" person, is his wife just being unreasonable if she objects to his fooling around? And does his personal popularity mean that, as a Christian, he is not committing a sin? Most people, if they take a moment to think about it, readily see that "niceness" does not really work as a test of ethics. I further believe that any church that bases its ethical teaching on sophisticated versions of such value systems is in deep trouble.

2. Is opposition to homosexual practice unloving?

If you believe that homosexual practice is unjust (against God's will and intention for humanity), then you must oppose it. Or, to put it in secular terms, if you understand that homosexual practice arises from a deeply rooted neurotic condition, and that it results in a HIV infection rate of from fifty percent to seventy-five percent of practising homosexuals, then you must offer help to active homosexuals to get out of that lifestyle before it kills them.

One path that many Christians with a homosexual orientation consider is to reorient themselves to a heterosexual orientation (attraction to suitable members of the opposite sex). Is this a realistic goal? For many homosexuals, it apparently is. But, unfortunately, some are discouraged from considering this by incorrect statements to the effect that such a reorientation is not even possible.

This type of situation is nothing new. When I began my ministry twenty-five years ago, most ministers and most psychiatrists despaired at the thought of helping practising alcoholics. Some still do. But when I developed a close relationship with a small struggling Alcoholics Anonymous (AA) group in Castlegar, B.C., I discovered that successes did occur frequently enough to keep us all hoping and to keep alcoholics trying. With much pain, and many a slip, "hopeless alcoholics" found sanity and a new life. In the past twenty-five years, AA has helped millions of suffering alcoholics in North America and around the world, in just such small groups as this.

Nowadays, with new insights from the social sciences,[†] groups such as Homosexuals Anonymous and Exodus International are following the spiritual, self-help, small group approach successfully pioneered by AA. These groups, along with caring psychotherapists, enjoy success at reorientation in thirty to sixty percent of cases, which is similar to, though higher than, that of alcoholism recovery under AA.

I believe that it is as unloving to tell a homosexual that his condition is natural and "a gift of God," as it is to say that to an alcoholic. Both are thereby condemned to a life of pain and ill

[†] This will be dealt with in Chapters 1 and 5.

health. This is not, as is naively assumed, because of adverse public opinion. The pain is caused by a deep intrapsychic conflict. The ill health is caused by putting parts of the body to uses for which they were never intended.

3. Does a theology that emphasizes "liberation" demand our approval of homosexual practice?

A theology that emphasizes "liberation" does not demand the approval of any activity not considered legitimate for Christians on Scriptural grounds. It does not demand the approval of homosexual practice any more than it demands the approval of adultery, incest, bestiality or pedophilia. For that matter, there is no way of interpreting Scripture so as to set aside condemnation of any one of these practices that could not also find a way to approve all of the others. To base the approval of homosexual practice on the claims and demands of gay rights activists is a betrayal of the proper Biblical basis for all theology.

All individuals in a pluralistic society should have protection of their civil rights. But this does not mean that Christians must approve of or agree with the opinions or actions of these individuals.

In some parts of this book an analogy will be drawn between alcoholism and homosexuality. As I indicated above, I have been involved with helping alcoholics for many years; that is the reason for my interest and background in this topic. A review of similarities and differences between the two problems is appropriate here, especially in the light of recent interest among scientists in studying possible genetic indications for alcoholism, homosexuality and other forms of behaviour.

Though the differences between alcoholism and homosexual orientation are significant, there are enough similarities to aid in our understanding of the causes of homosexual orientation:

– there is often, although not always, disruption in the family life of the family of origin.

– both problems have some aspects which are best understood using the concept of a disease and other aspects which are best understood using the concept of an addiction.

– both problems often seem to encourage in the individual a self-pitying, self-destructive character.

– both problems can be successfully treated. The successful treatment for alcoholism is abstinence. For homosexuality, it may be abstinence (celibacy) or reorientation. But the rate of successful treatment for homosexuality is higher (30-60 percent). This may be because there are two possible routes of treatment for homosexuality, not just one, a fact which improves the odds that at least one route will work.

– studies have shown that both alcoholism and homosexuality are almost non-existent in traditional, observant Jewish families. As with so many personal and social problems, strong faith and strong families may be the most sure form of prevention.

Before we begin, I want to briefly outline the structure of this book:

Chapter I examines the ideology of "gay rights" activists. The term "ideology" will be used in the sense in which it is defined in Webster's Dictionary as ". . . the integrated assertions, theories and aims constituting a politico-social program . . . with an implication of propagandizing. . . ." To what extent is the gay rights ideology based on fact?

Chapter II examines what homosexuals actually do and what effects these practices have on human health. I acknowledge that some readers will find this chapter very difficult reading. But it is necessary because there is a great deal of ignorance about this area – and a surprising amount of it is among people who claim to "see nothing wrong with" homosexual practices. Certainly, it will become apparent why homosexual lobbyists would prefer to discuss almost any subject other than typical homosexual behaviour.

Chapter III looks at the changes gay rights lobbyists seek to make in the law. They seek to change our society's understanding of human rights and of the family. What sort of "homosexual family" are they proposing for the future? Are such changes likely to occur in our society?

Chapter IV examines the teachings of the Scriptures on human sexuality. The traditional teachings will be compared with new interpretations proposed by homosexual rights activists. Who is right about what Scripture says about these practices?

Chapter V examines the revisions of language, theology and ethics which are proposed by the supporters of the gay rights activists. To what extent can they be accommodated in a Christian church?

Chapter VI looks at insights from modern psychology in order to help us understand the issues surrounding homosexual inclinations. The church is asked if she has the faith and love to do the costly things that are necessary to help suffering homosexuals.

Chapter VII asks if homosexuals are truly welcome in the church. Or do we have a double standard for sins?

This enlarged and updated version of my earlier book, *Trojan Horse*, would not have been possible without the wise advice and vital editorial work of Brian Stiller, executive director of the Evangelical Fellowship of Canada, and editors Audrey Dorsch and Denyse O'Leary.

My thanks to the members of North Lonsdale congregation and other committed lay people who read the early drafts of this material. My thanks also to the many ministers of Christian denominations who encouraged me with their prayers. And a special thanks to the many former homosexuals who have told me that this book has been helpful to them. Most especially, my gratitude and appreciation to my wife Margaret, who did all the typing with her characteristic encouragement, patience, and love.

D.F.

. . . the decisive word of Christian ethics must consist in a warning against entering upon the whole way of life which can only end in the tragedy of concrete homosexuality. We know that in its early stages it may have an appearance of particular beauty and spirituality. . . . What is needed is that the recognition of the divine command should cut sharply across the attractive beginnings. The real perversion takes place, the original decadence and disintegration begins, where man will not see his partner of the opposite sex and therefore the primal form of fellowman, . . . trying to be human in himself as sovereign man or woman. . . . For in this supposed discovery of the genuinely human, man and woman give themselves up to the worship of a false god.[1]

Karl Barth, *Church Dogmatics III, 4 1*

Is the homosexual issue in fact comparable to those other liberation movements of recent decades? At least in one very significant aspect, the answer is NO. Quite simply the Bible explicitly and repeatedly condemns homosexual acts . . . In this important aspect homosexuality must be viewed differently from other liberation movements.[2]

Arvid Adell, *The Christian Century*

CHAPTER ONE

Understanding Homosexual Orientation

Many ordinary church members are puzzled by the issues surrounding homosexuals in the church and in society that have become controversial in recent years. The homosexual rights movement in North America began to be active in New York in 1969. Its goal is the full social acceptance of homosexual practice as a viable, healthy, normal lifestyle on a par with sexual relationships between men and women. Its supporters lobby psychiatric, psychological, legal, political and religious organizations to achieve this goal of giving homosexuality equal status with heterosexuality. Hence the explosion of this issue within the churches of North America in recent years. The current strategy of homosexual rights activists is to present practising homosexuals as a morally neutral minority group similar to women or blacks who have been unfairly discriminated against and deserve special human rights status. Before we begin to determine how we, as Christians, should respond to this demand, we must first consider what specific point of view about homosexual orientation and practice we are being asked to accept.

The ideology generally supported by homosexual rights activists has five basic premises:[3]

1. Homosexual orientation (a preference for members of

one's own sex as sexual partners) is genetically or biologically based.

2. Homosexuals constitute at least ten percent of the population.

3. Homosexual practice (sodomy, or anal intercourse, primarily) is a healthy lifestyle which harms no one.

4. Homosexuals are no more prone to child sexual abuse (sometimes called pedophilia) than are heterosexuals. Therefore, any concern about homosexuals in this area is simply prejudice.

5. Homosexual orientation cannot be changed. Any suggestion that change can occur is based on a lack of acceptance of homosexuals.

It is worthwhile to examine these premises in some detail because many Christians will be deeply influenced in their thinking about homosexual orientation and practice by whether or not they believe all of them – or any of them – to be true.[†]

1. Homosexual orientation (a preference for members of one's own sex as sexual partners) is genetically or biologically based.

Some argue that a person with a homosexual orientation is "born gay", just as people are born blue-eyed or brown-eyed. According to many who believe this, homosexuals "cannot help" who they are or what they do. Therefore, the rejection of homosexual practice[††] by churches is similar to the oppression of blacks in South Africa by apartheid.

---

† However, as I will attempt to show in a later chapter, that may not be where the issue lies for us Christians anyway.

†† By "homosexual orientation" I mean a tendency to have feelings of sexual attraction to members of one's own sex. By "homosexual practice" I mean sodomy and other forms of sexual intercourse with a member of one's own sex. The distinction between orientation and practice is important for Christian ethics, as I will show later.

There are several issues to deal with here, but let us start with the question of fact: What is the latest verdict from scientific studies on homosexual orientation? Do we really know what causes people to prefer members of their own sex as sexual partners?

So far, the studies of chromosomes[4] and hormones[5] have not supported the theory of a biological basis for homosexual orientation. Indeed, it has yet to be demonstrated that individuals are born with any sexual orientation.

Some people claim, however, that studies have definitely demonstrated that people are "born gay" or that certain paths have been laid down in their brains before birth that determine their sexual orientation. The most frequently quoted source for these views is a study by Franz Kallmann, completed in 1952.[6] Out of a small sample of identical twins studied, in every case where one twin was homosexual, both twins were homosexual. Since identical twins share a genetic code, it was concluded that genetics was the cause of their homosexual orientation.[†]

The major weakness of this study is that these pairs of identical twins were raised together, which means that they also shared an environment. A common environment could have led both twins to have homosexual tendencies. This is a significant issue because the Freudian tradition of psychiatry, which has been the dominant one for most of this century, generally considers environmental issues to be the key factors in the development of homosexual orientation. (See Chapter 6 for a fuller discussion of psychiatric views on homosexuality.) Only a study of identical twins *separated at birth* could help unravel the genetic influences from the environmental ones.

There is another problem with the Kallmann study as well. Its findings have not been replicated in more than 40 years of subse-

[†] Identical twins occur when a fertilized egg splits in half and each half continues to develop as an embryo. The original fertilized egg had only one genetic code, and the resulting twins share it.

quent research. In science, if an experimental finding cannot be replicated, serious researchers are cautious about using the findings of the original research. There is too great a risk that an error may have been made in selecting the subjects or interpreting the data.

In December 1991 Michael Bailey and Richard Pillard published the results of their male twin studies.[7] In March of 1993 the same researchers reported on female twins. Their study, like the Kallmann research, did not focus on identical twins separated at birth. They found that fifty-two percent of the male pairs and forty-eight percent of the females were both homosexual, if one was homosexual. While the number of homosexual pairs is certainly high, it does not support a theory that homosexual orientation is simply "genetic" or "prenatal". The reason is that, among identical twins, one would expect the rate to be even higher, if genetics or prenatal experience were the only explanation. Why, for example, is it not the one hundred percent figure reported by Kallman? Unlike their non-twin sibs, identical twins have no genes or obstetrical history apart from each other. Rather, the fact that all pairs are *not* uniformly homosexual points to other factors at work in the development of homosexuality.

A more recent study in the *British Journal of Psychiatry* (March 1992) showed that only twenty percent of homosexual twins had homosexual co-twins. It concluded that "genetic factors are insufficient explanation of the development of sexual orientation".[8] Unfortunately, this study was virtually unreported in North America.

Another recent study that gained considerable publicity was reported by Simon LeVay, a neuroscientist in California. His study of 41 brain cadavers looked at an area of the hypothalamus, the part of the brain that regulates basic body functions such as temperature. This area, believed to govern sexual activity, was found to be smaller in homosexual men than in heterosexual men. However, the portion of the hypothalamus that

LeVay studied (the INAH3) is actually very difficult to measure. It is smaller than a snowflake and, even more problematic, scientists disagree as to *how* it should be measured. Should the volume of the region be measured or the number of neurons it contains? But a more basic problem also arises: Even if there is a difference in size, does that mean that size governs homosexuality or that homosexuality governs the size? No one is sure, according to neurophysiologist Kenneth Klivington.[9]

Klivington points out that "You could postulate that brain change occurs throughout life as a consequence of experience." He suggests that there may be a kind of "feedback loop" in which the brain influences behaviour, behaviour shapes experience, and experience affects the organization of the brain. This "non-linear" approach to biology and genetics, which results from advanced computer studies of the universe, suggests new directions for the discussion of these "nature vs. nurture" issues that a scientist of Kallmann's day never would have even considered. In this particular case, the problem is complicated by the fact that LeVay admits that he is not certain about the sexual histories of the persons whose brains he studied.

Another study, published in *Science* magazine in July 1993, gained a great deal of press coverage. This complicated study found that thirty-three pairs of homosexual brothers had a similar stretch of DNA in a region of the chromosome known as Xq28. The leader of the study, molecular biologist Dean Hamer, admitted that the failure of the study to find such a similarity in nearly 20 percent of the men studied shows "that you cannot just look at the DNA and predict who will or will not be gay".[10] Yet, some homosexual lobbyists claimed that this "proved" the genetic basis of homosexuality. It should be remembered that in the past three years scientists have announced a genetic basis for manic-depression, alcoholism and schizophrenia with great fanfare, only to have to retract later. One of these scientists, Miron Baron, a behavioural geneticist at Columbia University who made such a retraction about a manic-depression gene, said that "given the complexity of homosexuality, the statistical strength of the study, while intriguing, is not overwhelming".[11]

However, William Byrne, resident of psychiatry at Columbia University's College of Physicians and Surgeons, comments that "If you look at any one piece of that 'born gay' evidence, it is inconclusive. It's like trying to add up a hundred zeros so you can get one".[12]

One reason that the genetic (and prenatal) arguments for the cause of homosexuality are inconclusive is that no one has been able to show that there is a set of genetic or prenatal circumstances under which homosexuality will certainly occur. However, as Dr. Byrne has commented, "The public is now getting the impression that there's this mountain of evidence being built to support the idea that homosexuality is biological. But in fact what we're seeing is a stream of zeros being added together".[13]

The reason for the sudden interest in genetic explanations for homosexuality, apart from enthusiastic support by gay rights activists, is that "genetic" explanations for various social phenomena are currently popular. The June 1993 *Scientific American* comments, "Eugenics is back in fashion. The message that genetics can explain, predict and even modify human behavior for the betterment of society is promulgated not just on sensationalistic talk shows but by our most prominent scientists."[14]

The main reason for this popularity is the remarkable success of biologists in mapping human genes in recent years, which raises hopes that many age-old questions will be answered. Also, certain types of political activists (gay rights activists, for example) hope that new findings will bolster their cause. It is worth pointing out that the demand (it really amounts to that) by militant homosexuals that their behaviour be accepted as a "genetic" condition is politically necessary, since that credo is what cements the homosexual rights groups' self-identification with blacks and women. This self-identification is authentic only if homosexual orientation is indeed "in the genes". But if it is established that homosexual orientation has a number of causes, some genetic and some environmental, and that it is subject to personal choice in the sense that a person could change sexual orientation if desired, the impetus of a powerful special interest group would begin to dissipate.

The article in *Scientific American* notes,

> Critics contend that no good can come of bad science. Far from moving inexorably closer to its goals, they point out, the field of behavioral genetics is mired in the same problems that have always plagued it. Behavioral traits are extraordinarily difficult to define, and practically every claim of a genetic basis can also be explained as an environmental effect.[15]

Jonathan Beck, a geneticist at Harvard University, comments, "This has been a huge enterprise, and for the most part the work has been done shoddily. Even careful people get sucked into misinterpreting data."[16]

Future research is unlikely to discover genetic features that govern homosexual orientation absolutely, but it may demonstrate some features that predispose a given person to it. However, what this will – or will not – establish is another matter, to which I will return later.

Some people have argued that homosexual behaviour exists in every culture, and that therefore there must be something "biological" or "natural" about it. Now, it is not strictly true that homosexual behaviour is found in every culture. Researcher R.T. Barnhouse points out that in certain cultures, such as traditional China and the Israeli kibbutz, homosexuality is virtually unknown.[17] In any case, worldwide studies by social commentator Arno Karlen come to this conclusion:

> . . . we do know that predominant or exclusive homosexuality is seen *negatively everywhere*, and that when a society alleged to approve of homosexuality is carefully

> studied, it turns out that *homosexual acts are accepted only in special situations or times of life*, and to the extent that they do not impair heterosexual functioning or loss of sexual identity. . . . Whenever the final limits of heterosexuality and biologically appropriate role are infringed, the result is sanctions that range from death through persecution to harassment and mild contempt.[18]

Actually, there is no evidence of a civilization that has accepted homosexuality as a normal lifetime alternative to heterosexuality. If our civilization decides to do so, it will be the first in history.

Some people claim that homosexual practice is a "natural" biologically based behaviour for human beings because they believe it to be a common type of behaviour among animals. Usually they base their argument on the "mounting" behaviour of domesticated pets who "mount" other animals or even people without regard to gender (or will even mount objects). The researcher most often quoted in this area is Frank Beach. In 1949, he wrote an article indicating that homosexuality was common in the animal world. But in 1965, on the basis of further research, he specifically denied his earlier views. (Despite this reversal of opinion, C.A. Tripp, in *The Homosexual Matrix*, quotes Beach's earlier views and ignores his reversal – even though Tripp's bibliography listed Beach's later writings. This is an example of the difficulties that one encounters in trying to sort out data in this area.) R.T. Barnhouse summarizes the behaviour of animals as follows:

> . . . in the animal kingdom there is no such thing as homosexual behaviour which includes climax or even, between males, intromission. The rare exceptions occur under the extreme circumstances of artificial stress, such as overcrowding of rats in laboratories.[19]

Barnhouse also comments:

> What observers of animals frequently mistake for homo-

> sexuality is actually part of a very elaborate dominant/submissive ritual behaviour. When any animal attacks another of the same species, the animal who is losing the fight turns some weaker part of his anatomy toward the aggressor. Wolves, for instance, turn their heads to expose the jugular vein, at which point the fight is over as the loser has conceded the victory. In primates it is common to expose the usually highly-coloured buttocks or the genitals as a signal of defeat. These gestures are not sexual; they have no connection with sexual arousal, orgasm, or reproduction.[20]

Certainly, biologists have observed a "learned" homosexuality in imprisoned or stressed animals. But as F.A. Beach observed, "I don't know of any authenticated instance of males or females in the animal world (in a non-captive state) preferring a homosexual partner."[21] This is not really a very surprising finding, since such behaviour would undermine the survival of a species.

If homosexual orientation is "genetic" or "biological", what are we to make of the established fact that many homosexuals become heterosexual, often as a result of psychological therapies? (See Chapter VI, section on successful treatment, for a detailed discussion of this subject.) The fact that sexual orientation can be changed at all argues against a simple genetic or biological explanation of homosexual orientation.

What do homosexuals themselves think? Although many homosexual rights activists insist that homosexual orientation is genetic in origin, a large-scale survey of self-declared, practising homosexuals revealed that fewer than fifteen percent felt they had been born that way.[22]

In conclusion, the sciences simply do not provide evidence that homosexual orientation occurs as a result of genetics or biology. In the future, a genetic or biological component may be

† Sexual intercourse with an animal.

demonstrated. But such evidence would not prove that homosexual behaviour is a necessary result, or that churches should accept homosexual behaviour as appropriate for Christians.

2. Homosexuals constitute at least ten percent of the population.

This commonly used figure of "ten percent" is usually quoted in order to show that homosexuality is a widespread natural phenomenon. It is derived from the "Kinsey report" published in 1948. This report, entitled *Sexual Behavior in the Human Male* (Alfred Kinsey, Wardell Pomeroy and Clyde Martin), claimed to describe "statistically common behaviour" in the population of the United States in the 1940s. It received considerable publicity because it reported high rates of promiscuity in the population and far higher rates of homosexual practice – and bestiality† – than people had expected.

Kinsey's reports had great social impact because they purported to be truly *scientific* studies, as opposed to what he considered to be the prejudiced thinking of society.[23] He found that thirty-seven percent of all males have homosexual experiences between adolescence and old age. According to his findings, ten percent of white American males are "more or less exclusively homosexual" for at least three years between the ages of sixteen and fifty-five; eight percent are "exclusively homosexual" for the same period; and four percent are exclusively homosexual throughout their lives. One may well wonder why the ten percent figure (which covers only three years) is frequently quoted rather than the four percent figure (which refers to lifetime homosexuals). It is generally agreed that transient homosexual desires or homosexual practices do not mean that a person will necessarily have a lifelong homosexual orientation. But there are other serious questions to be asked concerning both Kinsey's research methods and the sample of population he used.

One problem is that his research method did *not* involve a scientific sample of a cross-section of the population. His data was gathered from volunteers. Kinsey was actually warned about the inaccuracy of data gathered from volunteers by the eminent psychologist, Abraham Maslow. Maslow, who had done sex research before Kinsey, cautioned that those who volunteer for sex research tend to be more aggressive and deviant in their sexual behaviour than typical non-volunteers. Maslow even demonstrated this to Kinsey by using his classes at Brooklyn College in an experiment. Maslow later wrote, "As I expected, the volunteer error was proven and the whole basis for Kinsey's statistics was proven to be shaky. But he refused to publish it and refused even to mention it in his books. . . ."[24]

Quite apart from this "volunteer error", which is a significant problem in any type of sex research, Kinsey also failed to exercise the reasonable caution of making sure that all his volunteers were acquired from the general population. Kinsey's colleagues have revealed that up to twenty-five percent of the men that he used to find out what constituted "normal" sexual behaviour were current or former prison inmates. Among this group, some forty-four percent had had "homosexual experience in prison".[25] Another large group were 1,200 persons convicted of sex offences, whose experiences are part of Kinsey's "statistically common behaviour". Clearly, these individuals cannot have had "statistically common" behaviour.

The 1993 *Janus Report on Sexual Behavior*[26] (named after its authors, S.S. Janus and C.L. Janus, not the two-faced Roman god of the same name) updates the Kinsey research. Although the Janus research does not over-represent the prison population, it tends to over-represent highly educated, single, upper-income subjects. It also under-represents Jews by a factor of five and over-represents "other religions" by a factor of four.[27] The Janus researchers report only twenty-two percent of men as having (ever) had a homosexual experience. They note that although gay activist groups use the ten percent figure derived from

Kinsey, their own research obtains a figure for self-identified homosexuals of four percent for men and two percent for women, for a national average of less than three percent.[28]

Other recent studies indicate that from one to four percent of the population are consistently homosexually inclined.[29] A 1989 study from the University of Chicago showed a rate of exclusive homosexuality of less than one percent. A British study reported even lower figures in 1989: that only 1.7 percent of a randomly selected group of males had *ever* had homosexual intercourse and less than *half* of that group had had it more than once.[30]

To determine the proportion of the population that may properly be considered "homosexual", we need to establish how many adults maintain a pattern of homosexual orientation and behaviour throughout life, rather than just experiencing two or three episodes in a lifetime. Though statistics differ from study to study, it is apparent that researchers studying typical adults are not coming up with findings of anything like ten percent of the population. They are generally having results in the one to two percent range.

The only reason that this battle of statistics should concern us is that the commonly used "ten percent" figure, which has no basis in fact, is frequently cited in the popular media as a sort of unalterable law. This carelessness with facts and figures should serve as a warning that truth can be the first casualty in a propaganda campaign. We need to be cautious about what we believe.

3. Homosexual practice (sodomy or anal intercourse primarily) is a healthy lifestyle which harms no one.

It is generally acknowledged that homosexuals can be mature and healthy in many parts of their lives. The question is whether adult homosexual orientation and practice are, in themselves healthy. Homosexual rights advocates have found psychologists who advance the view that the lifestyle of the practising homosexual is healthy and harms no one. For example, seeking to establish that practising homosexuals are well-adjusted, psychologist Evelyn Hooker undertook research to question negative stereotypes about them. She sought to compare the psychological adjustment of a group of heterosexuals with a group of homosexuals. But she did not choose a random sample. She chose her sample of homosexuals from persons recommended to her by homosexual organizations who wished to put their most admirable members forward. Then she removed from this group anyone who struck her as obviously pathological. And then, according to psychiatrist Marjorie Rosenberg,[31]

> Additional limitations to the validity of the research were introduced through her criteria of adjustment, performance on the Rorschach and two other projective tests. These tests are generally used to augment rather than to make a diagnosis and are not intended to be used by examiners who have not seen the subject. The Rorschach, in particular, has shown to be an extremely unreliable tool, varying as much with the personality of the tester as with that of the subject, and frequently unable to distinguish men from women; let alone homosexuals from heterosexuals.

Hooker came to be considered an expert on homosexuality, however, and by the end of the 1960s she headed the American National Institute of Mental Health Task Force on Homosexuality.

The influence of Kinsey and Hooker was partly responsible for the victory of the gay rights activists when the American Psychiatric Association in 1973 removed homosexuality from the list of disorders in the *Manual of Psychiatric Disorders*. It was replaced by the classification "sexual orientation disturbance" which applied only to those who were disturbed by or wished to change their sexual orientation. It should be noted that, despite the ruling, psychiatrists were far from agreed on this subject. A special task force of experts who spent many years working with homosexuals conducted an in-depth investigation of the subject, but their findings were ignored. Many experts believe that the APA decision was more political than scientific.[32]

A more recent survey of psychiatric opinion was conducted by the journal *Medical Aspects of Human Sexuality* in 1977. Twenty-five hundred psychiatrists responded. Of this group, sixty-nine percent held that homosexual men were less capable of "mature loving relationships" than heterosexual men. Seventy percent of the 2,500 asserted that the problems of homosexuals were the result of personal conflicts rather than society's stigmatization. This negative view of the healthiness of homosexuality is reflected in the continuing categorization of homosexuality as a "mental disorder" by the World Health Organization. This reflects worldwide, not just North American, psychiatric opinion.

What about the social evidence? It is established that high rates of suicide, promiscuity, alcoholism, drug abuse and venereal disease are characteristic of the homosexual lifestyle. The rapid spread of AIDS (fifty percent to seventy-five percent infection rate) is a tragic commentary on the extraordinary promiscuity that is associated with homosexual practice. Pro-homosexual sociologists Alan Bell and Martin Weinberg reported that their research revealed that only nine percent of homosexual males had fewer than twenty-five different sexual partners in their lifetime. Thirty-two percent had between one hundred and five hundred; fifteen percent had between five hundred and one thousand; and twenty-eight percent reported more than one thousand different partners. Only one percent reported lifetime monogamous relationships.[33] Bell reports that the modal white male homosexual claimed 1,000 or more sexual partners during a lifetime, ". . . most of whom were strangers prior to their sexual meeting and with whom sexual activity occurred only once. Only a few of these partners were persons for whom there was much care or affection or were ever seen socially again".[34] Forty-three percent of white male homosexuals reported "cruising" for sexual contacts once a week or more.

And more than one third "cruised" once a month or less. They cruised in gay bars, steam baths, streets, private parties, parks and beaches, public toilets and movie theatres, in that order.

The "drivenness" or addictive aspect of homosexuality that expresses itself in this degree of promiscuity is thought by many to be characteristic of a neurotic compulsion.[35] This is so much the case that the German sociologist Dannecker, himself a professed homosexual, bluntly declared that "faithful homosexual friendship" is a myth.[36]

The serious social problems outlined above make it clear that the choice of an active homosexual lifestyle contains many costs and risks that would not otherwise be factors; hence, it cannot really be said to be a healthy lifestyle that harms no one. In a later chapter, we will look at the specifically medical problems that homosexual practice can create.

4. Homosexuals are no more prone to child sexual abuse (sometimes called pedophilia) than are heterosexuals. Therefore, any concern about homosexuals in this area is simply prejudice.

Child sexual abuse and molestation are too serious a problem for any church to ignore. For one thing, too many of the child victims have been harmed in church-related institutions or on church property, as recent well-publicized incidents show. Even at the risk of being accused of prejudice, it is necessary for the church to ask hard questions about child sexual abuse, with a view to protecting children better in the future than they have sometimes been protected in the past. Some of the questions may be unpopular but they cannot be avoided.

One aspect of the problem, which has been ignored until recent years, is the abuse of male children by adult men. Many researchers are now finding that boys are as frequently abused as girls.[37] One English study found that boys made up three-quarters of the children abused.[38]

It has been argued, for example by sociologist Richard Knudten, that heterosexuals are more prone to molest children than are homosexuals because only thirty to forty-five percent of all sexual offenses committed against children under fourteen were homosexual molestation.[39] But if homosexuals constitute only ten percent of the population at the outside, then they are very disproportionately involved in child sexual abuse. And, if the estimates of more modern research (which consistently gives a lower figure for lifetime homosexuals) are accepted, homosexual involvement in thirty to forty-five percent of crimes against children is quite remarkable.

A recent survey indicated that seventy-three percent of homosexuals admitted having sex with boys sixteen to nineteen years old or younger.[40] The director of a sex offender program reported that eighty-five percent of pedophiles had been sexually abused as children.[41] Another author claims that boys who were victimized by older men were four times more likely to engage in homosexual activity as adults than were non-victims.[42]

Of course, most homosexuals are not sexually attracted to children. But current research points to homosexual pedophilia as a widespread problem that has only recently come to public attention. It is not simply prejudice against homosexuals that causes church institutions to have concerns in this area; until more light can be shed on the specific circumstances under which sexual molestation of children occurs, it would be irresponsible not to raise the issue about an apparently high rate of sexual abuse of boys by adult practising homosexuals.

5. Homosexual orientation cannot be changed. Any suggestion that change can occur is based on a lack of acceptance of homosexuals.

Another commonly heard theme is that homosexual orientation cannot be changed. This rests in turn upon the assumption that homosexual orientation is "in the genes", which, as we have seen, has not been established. But anyone who claims that sexual orientation cannot be changed labours under a very heavy burden of proof: even one instance of a changed sexual orientation would falsify the proposition.

The fact is that change is quite common in this area. Many psychotherapists and counsellors can provide case histories of persons of homosexual orientation who have moved into a heterosexual orientation.[43] (Incidentally, most claim to lead a happier life with a heterosexual orientation.) The rate around the world for change using a variety of approaches ranges from thirty to sixty percent. Of course, these figures apply only to persons who were unhappy enough as practising (or non-practising) homosexuals to attempt such a change. But, as we have seen above, the fact of these persons' existence calls into question the simple dictums of the gay rights activists ("Homosexuality is in the genes. It cannot be changed."). Instead, a complex pattern of behaviour is revealed, subject in some part – perhaps in large part – to personal choice.

Some gay rights activists claim that the emphasis that churches lay on the possibility of change reveals a lack of acceptance of homosexuals. But this is misguided. It is cruel, not loving, to tell homosexuals that they were born that way and no change is possible, when there is considerable evidence to the contrary. Apart from the serious ethical issues that homosexual behaviour entails for the Christian (which I will discuss in a later chapter), the practising homosexual lifestyle is a high-risk lifestyle, particularly where men are concerned. For many people, the moral reasons for wanting to change are intertwined with some very practical issues of personal survival. The fact that help to change is available to the homosexual means that all morally serious Christians must see that this help is made known – although we do acknowledge the risk that some individuals will be offended by any information about changing a homosexual orientation.

Conclusion

As the discussion above shows, not one of the five assertions stated at the beginning of this chapter has been proven. In fact, the evidence is mostly against them. However, many churches have been actively lobbied to incorporate these assertions into their teachings about homosexual orientation and practice and to state that homosexual practice is not morally wrong. If a church wishes to say, despite all evidence and despite the clear teaching of Scripture, that homosexual practice is equal to marriage, then it can do so. Such a church can claim, perhaps, a new revelation, a new paradigm, a new cutting edge of intuition. But it cannot do so without rejecting reason, Scripture and 2,000 years of Christian tradition.

Study Guide Questions

1. "Eugenics is back in fashion. The message that genetics can explain, predict and even modify human behavior . . . is promulgated not just on sensationalistic talk shows but by our most prominent scientists." (quotation from *Scientific American*)

Can you think of desires and behaviour other than homosexuality about which some people are proclaiming, "I can't help it! It's in my genes." Do you think that there might be a hidden payoff in making such an apparently depressing claim about one's behaviour? How should a Christian respond?

2. "Even careful people get sucked into misinterpreting data." (quotation from geneticist Jonathan Beck about data on genetic predispositions to behaviour)

Why do you think that even careful people might be fooled in this particular area?

3. ". . . the commonly used 'ten percent' figure, frequently cited in the popular media [as the number of lifetime homosexuals in the population], has no basis in fact."

In this and many other areas, media sources have been known to rely on data that can easily be shown to be false. Why do you think they do this? Is it just laziness or is there a hidden payoff? Would there be risks in probing for the truth in certain cases? What might the risks be?

4. ". . . a church might claim, perhaps, a new revelation, a new paradigm, a new cutting edge of intuition."

Can there be a truly new revelation for Christians? How might it occur? What sort of a revelation might it be? Could it be in direct conflict with Scripture? With reason? With tradition? With an almost unanimous Christian public opinion? Discuss.

I have treated hundreds of homosexuals. None of them, deep down, thought he was normal. Simulating eating is not eating. Simulating being female is not being female. Simulating sex is not sex.[1]

Dr. Armand Nicholai,
Chief psychiatrist, Medical School at Harvard University

Those who urge the acceptance of homosexuality as a normal form of sexuality, rather than a behaviourial disorder, developmental arrest or failure, or a clinical illness, reflect the blurred boundaries of social behaviour which currently impair communal health in many ways.[2]

Dr. Charles Socarides,
Clinical Professor of Psychiatry,
Albert Einstein College of Medicine,
New York City

Most studies have found that among homosexual and bisexual men the prevalence of HIV infection ranges from fifty percent to seventy-five percent.[3]

Masters and Johnson

CHAPTER TWO

What Do Homosexuals Do?

If there is one subject that the homosexual lobby usually does not want discussed, it is the question of what precisely homosexuals do that gives rise to so much censure and disgust. You would think, from the public rhetoric, that they simply want men to be able to express their friendships openly by holding hands as they watch the sunset. But holding hands is *not* what the "gay lifestyle" is about. The gay lifestyle is about what homosexuals do with their *genitals* – and with other parts of the body not designed to be genitals but used by them for that purpose. These practices are both objectively unnatural and unhealthy, and also carry a very high personal and social cost. Some readers may be offended by the following descriptions, but in the interests of truth and clarity, we must proceed.

A Description of Homosexual Practices

Perhaps a medical description of homosexual practices would be the clearest way to explain them. The natural climax of sexual intercourse between a man and a woman involves the insertion of the penis of the man into the vagina of the woman prior to ejaculation (the emission of sperm). It is obvious that this step is essential for procreation to take place. Because male homosexuals possess only male sexual parts, they must find some alternative to the natural form of sexual intercourse, which requires the woman's parts as well. Though homosexuals may begin with manual masturbation, they soon move on to the more esoteric practices described by Dr. Bernard J. Klamecki in his excellent article titled "Medical Perspective of the Homosexual Issue."[4]

> Male homosexuals engage in a number of sexual practices that could lead to health problems. Most common is anal intercourse (sodomy), whereby the penis is inserted into the recipient's anus. This practice is not limited to male homosexuals but is also performed in heterosexual relationships as a birth control method or variant sexual position. Both the anal receiver or passive partner and the anal inserter or active partner can experience orgasm.
>
> Foreign objects are often used in order to produce a different erotic sensation or to instigate a more violent sexual activity (sadomasochism). Objects that I have removed from the rectum and lower bowel include corn cobs, light bulbs, vibrators, soda bottles, and varied wooden sticks.
>
> "Fisting" is when a fisted hand is inserted into the rectum, sometimes as far as the elbow, which produces varied sexually exciting sensations, strongly linking eroticism with pain. This practice is usually performed while under the influence of LSD, marijuana, cocaine or nitrites.
>
> Oral intercourse (fellatio) is when the penis is inserted into a recipient's mouth and is therefore not necessarily restricted to homosexuals. The physical problems that result include tearing of the tongue, lining of the mouth and upper throat, and bite marks to the penis.
>
> Rimming (anilingus) is when the tongue is used to lick or tickle the outlet of the rectum for sexual excitement, arousing, or foreplay. Needless to say, bacteria may con-

> taminate and infect the mouth. One other sexual practice is "Water Sports", in which urinating into the mouth or rectum is used as a sexual stimulant.
>
> Physical damage to the rectum may occur because of some of these practices. For example, because of the push/pull motion by a fairly hard, almost $1\frac{3}{4}$- to 2-inch diameter object (whether penis or foreign object) into the opening not designed to receive such an object, damage to the opening and its surrounding structure can occur. There is an antinatural activity being performed when the rectum is the recipient of a penis or foreign object. Because of this activity, cracking of the tissue (fissuring), open sores (ulcers), boils (abscesses), and other infections can occur in the skin of the surrounding tissues.
>
> If rectal penetration is a frequent activity, the recipient's rectal muscles may be injured and weakened, causing poor bowel or gas control. If the activity is violent, as in fisting or the use of large rough foreign objects, the walls of the rectum or lower bowel may be perforated. Persistent anal-rectal sexual activity can lead to various precancerous lesions such as Bowen's disease and Kaposi's sarcoma. Whenever tissues are traumatized, cracked, or abraded, they are vulnerable to bacterial infection.

The problem is that so much homosexual activity centres on the anus. God made the female vagina to consist of a type of tissue that stretches to receive the penis and, when necessary, to permit the passage of an infant. But the human anus was not intended to be subjected to such activity. It is made of a different type of tissue, which is easily torn. In addition, the mixing of blood, semen, feces and pre-existing sexually transmitted diseases is a recipe for the spread of disease. The fact that over ninety percent of homosexual men sometimes engage in anal sodomy, and seventy-five percent engage in it regularly, and that ninety percent of male and sixty-five percent of female homosexuals report oral/anal sex explains the high disease rate among practicing homosexuals.[5]

What Diseases Result from Homosexual Practices?

What are the results of these sexual practices? In the first place, the rate of illness in the homosexual community is legendary. Surveys have revealed that nearly eighty percent of homosexuals have suffered at least once from a sexually transmitted disease.[6] Although they comprise only one to two percent of the population, homosexuals account for half of the nation's cases of syphilis, gonorrhea of the throat, and of intestinal infections.[7] Homosexuals have a rate of infectious hepatitis B that is twenty to fifty times greater than that of heterosexual males. Some studies have shown that as many as one-half to three-quarters of homosexual men have or have had hepatitis B.[8] This serious, and sometimes fatal, disease presents a major public health problem.

Homosexual men can also develop a wide range of rare bowel diseases that are not often seen in the temperate zone, although they sometimes occur naturally in the tropics. Because so many-homosexual men ingest fecal matter, it is estimated that forty to fifty percent have parasitic amoebiasis, a parasitic disease of the colon.[9] These problems are so common among homosexuals that they have been described as the "gay bowel syndrome."

How seriously have these diseases been taken by "gay lifestyle" activists? Listen to these words by homosexual author, Randy Shilts:

> In San Francisco, two-thirds of gay men had suffered the debilitating disease [hepatitis B]. It was now proven statistically that a gay man had one chance in five of being infected with hepatitis B virus within 12 months of stepping off the bus into a typical urban gay scene. Within five years, infection was a virtual certainty.

> Another problem was enteric diseases, like amebiasis and giardiasis, caused by organisms that lodge themselves in the intestinal tracts of gay men with alarming frequency. At the New York Gay Men's Health Project, where Dan Williams was medical director, 30 percent of the patients suffered from gastrointestinal parasites. In San Francisco, incidence of "Gay Bowel Syndrome", as it was called in the medical journals, had increased by 8,000 percent after 1973. Infection with these parasites was a likely effect of anal intercourse, which was apt to put a man in contact with his partner's fecal matter, and was virtually a certainty through the then-popular practice of rimming, which medical journals politely called oral-anal intercourse.
>
> What was so troubling was that *nobody in the gay community seemed to care about these waves of infection.*[10]

Sexually transmitted diseases, hepatitis B and "gay bowel syndrome" are all serious health problems that are not merely the private concern of homosexuals. It is simply not the case that what consenting homosexuals do in a park, public washroom, or their own bedroom does not affect anyone but themselves. They present a major public health problem. So far, we have not even mentioned AIDS, which, unlike some of the infections cited above, has received widespread publicity as a deadly venereal disease. Some seventy to eighty percent of the AIDS cases in North America occur among practising homosexuals. Sexologists Masters and Johnson observe, "Most studies have found that among homosexual and bisexual men, the prevalence of HIV infection ranges from fifty percent to seventy-five percent".[11] Despite educational campaigns about AIDS and rhetoric to the effect that the homosexual community has changed its behaviours, a San Francisco study showed that more than seventy-five percent of homosexuals continued to practice anal sex.

More than seventy-five percent of these men did not use condoms regularly. And, although all these men knew people who had died of AIDS, more than half of their sexual partners were total strangers. They averaged 26.9 partners per year.[12]

The continuation of promiscuous anal sex in a deadly epidemic is incredibly irresponsible. Just as irresponsible is the denial that many homosexual activists exhibit toward AIDS testing as a preventive measure. For example, Troy Perry, founder of the homosexual church (Metropolitan Community Church or MCC), advises his friends *not* to be tested. He says,

> I presume we've all been exposed to the virus. I just take the attitude every gay man has been exposed to the virus, but I refuse to go down there and have my name in some computer somewhere. They will drag me away to give me any kind of test. . . . I've refused to take the test. I tell all of my friends, I'll take the test the day they have the treatment. . . . I just encourage my friends not to do it. They don't need the extra stress in their lives.[13]

What Other Sexual Practices May Be Involved in the Gay Lifestyle?

In welcoming homosexuals from around the world to the Gay Games in Vancouver in 1990, Svend Robinson, a homosexual MP, mentioned the wide variety of gay groups including cross-dressers and sado-masochists. He stressed the "inclusiveness" of the gay community. This "celebration of the diversity of our community" was even described as a "family event" by one of its organizers because it demonstrated an inclusivity like that of a family.

The homosexual lobby uses the ambiguous word "inclusive" a good deal. The implication is that it is good to include everything and bad to exclude anything. But what might this mean where sexual mores and practices are concerned?

"Inclusiveness," as it is used in this context, generally means that anything that contributes to sexual gratification, on whatever level, is good, and that any form of behaviour that can be classified as sexual should be affirmed and celebrated. There is no such thing as fulfilment – or perversion – of nature, or goals for sexual maturity. It is questionable whether moral values of any kind survive in such an atmosphere. People are believed to have a basic human right to whatever sexual experience they choose, and society is expected to change in whatever way is necessary to facilitate these rights.

What some activists are asking is this: Why should this "self-fulfilment," "choice" and "freedom" be withheld from children? The North American Man/Boy Love Association, (NAMBLA) carries this logic to its natural conclusion. Consider these statements from NAMBLA:[14]

- NAMBLA takes the view that sex is good, that homosexuality is good not only for adults, but for young people as well. We support all consensual sexual relationships regardless of age. As long as the relationship is mutually pleasurable and no one's rights are violated, sex should be no one else's business.
- Sexual liberation cannot be achieved without the liberation of children. This means many things. Children need to gain control over their lives, a control which they are denied on all sides. They need to break the yoke of "protection" which alienates them from themselves, a "protection" imposed on them by adults – their family, the schools, the state, and prevailing sexual and social mores.
- There is no age at which a person becomes capable of consenting to sex. The age of sexual consent is just one of many ways in which adults impose their system of control on children. . . . The state is the enemy of freedom, not its guarantor. The best evidence against the argument that children cannot consent to sex, including with adults, is the fact that millions do it anyway.

Of course, some might argue that NAMBLA's views are irrelevant because it is a tiny fringe organization. But this objection overlooks the fact that there are many pedophiles in the world and most of them are not members of NAMBLA – though NAMBLA clarifies their outlook by giving it a voice. The truth is that many homosexuals are attracted to boys because of their youth and innocence. A survey done by two homosexual authors revealed that three-fourths of homosexuals had had sex with boys sixteen to nineteen or younger. One reported, "My lover and I are into young boys 13-18 years old. . . . I am actively involved with many of them insofar as the social services, family courts, schools, probation departments, etc. are concerned". Yet another lamented,

> "How long will we boy lovers have to wait? How long before we can walk honestly and proudly hand-in-hand with our young friends and not have to palm them off as our nephews and stepsons?"[15]

The rhetoric of honesty, pride, rights, freedom and liberation serves the cause of pedophilia just as well as that of homosexual practice between consenting adults. In many countries, the age of consent is 14. It is now only 12 in the Netherlands. Is it possible that some "rights" campaign in the not-too-distant future will get the age lowered to 10, or 8, or removed all together?

Why Gay Activist Groups want to Shift the Focus away from Behaviour

How have the gay activist lobby groups been so successful in promoting the homosexual ideology? They have been successful because they have been able to draw public attention away from the unnatural, unhealthy and immoral behaviours described above that mark their sexual disorientation. Have you ever seen a newspaper report or television discussions of exactly *why* fifty to seventy-five percent of homosexuals are infected with the AIDS virus? As one of the leading interpreters of the "gay rights movement" Dennis Altman says,

> The greatest single victory of the gay movement over the past decade has been to shift the debate from behaviour to identity, thus forcing opponents into a position where they can be seen as attacking the civil rights of homosexual citizens rather than attacking specific and (as they see it) antisocial behaviour.[16]

By focusing on homosexual "identity" or "orientation," the homosexual lobby and their sexual liberation allies have, according to U.S. Congressman William Dannemyer, established certain "facts" which must be unquestionably accepted if one is to be allowed to speak authoritatively on this question.[17]

> "The facts" were simple: (1) homosexuality was predetermined before birth; (2) homosexuals had no choice over what they were or how they behaved; and (3) environmental factors, including the presence and attentions of homosexuals, could not affect a child adversely and *cause* homosexuality.
>
> The conclusions derived from these "facts" were inevitable: (1) like blacks, homosexuals were victims of ignorance and prejudice; (2) they needed protection from the persecution of the majority; and (3) laws had to be passed with this objective.

We have already seen in Chapter 1 that none of these politically correct "facts" has the merit of truth; they are a public relations campaign bought by the media. And the success of the propaganda campaign makes any public discussion of the truth or falsehood of these assertions difficult to sustain.

In the next chapter, we will turn to how homosexual activists are working to change the laws.

Study Guide Questions

1. Were you disturbed by what you read in Chapter 2? Would this kind of information make you less likely to befriend a fellow Christian who told you that he is gay? If so, how should you deal with your feelings?

2. Does awareness of these realities help us understand what is meant by "costly love"? Explain.

3. If your church starts a ministry to persons involved in the gay lifestyle, what qualities will it need? What problems will it have to overcome? Do you see yourself playing a role? What role?

4. What do you see as the role of prayer in such a ministry? Would it simply be the appropriate thing for Christians to do or would it be an essential component of the enterprise? Explain.

5. Do you have a private rank order of sins (by seriousness) in your own mind? Where do you place the sins to which you personally are most susceptible? How do you think Jesus would respond to your rank order if you presented it to Him?

The greatest single victory of the gay movement over the past decade has been to shift the debate from behavior to identity, thus forcing opponents into a position where they can be seen as attacking the civil rights of homosexual citizens rather than attacking specific and (as they see it) antisocial behavior.

Homosexual historian, Dennis Altman[1]

The main thing is to talk about gayness until the issue becomes thoroughly tiresome . . . . *In the early stages of the campaign, the public should not be shocked and repelled by premature exposure to homo*sexual *behavior itself. Instead the imagery of sex per se should be downplayed, and the issue of gay rights reduced, as far as possible, to an abstract social question . . . gays must be portrayed as victims in need of protection. . . .*

Homosexual authors, Marshall Kirk
and Hunter Madsen[2]

CHAPTER THREE

Homosexuality and the Law

The same division of opinion exists in regard to the causes of homosexual practice as to the causes of alcoholism. In both cases, some scientists argue that the genetic component is the determining factor as to who develops the tendency, while others insist that the psychological aspects are more important. Yet no one argues that drunkenness is "normal," that alcoholics have "no choice," that alcoholism should be accepted as an "alternative lifestyle" and a "natural and civil right" or that no treatment should be offered.

Yet homosexual lobby groups make all these claims for themselves and constantly compare themselves, as a group, to women and blacks. They are, of course, intentionally confusing the *condition* of being a woman or a man, a white or a black, with the unhealthy *sexual behaviour* of homosexuals. In the area of law, homosexual lobbyists want to be viewed as a genetically determined group in need of protection in the same way as women or blacks. As individual men and women, they have the same rights as other individual men and women, of course. So what they are really asking for are special privileges based on their sexual *behaviour*. They want other citizens who find their sexual behaviour repugnant, because it is so objectively unnatural and unhealthy, to be forced to accept it, to support it, and even to encourage it.

Sexual Orientation As A Human Right: What Will It Mean in Practice?

The homosexual lobby demands protection for its sexual *orientation*. For example, they want discrimination on the basis of "sexual orientation" to be included in human rights legislation as a prohibited ground of discrimination. But what is "sexual orientation"? Is it not a personal sexual attraction to something?

If psychological "orientation" is the condition for which protection is sought, then just which orientations are to be protected? All of them? Or just some of them? Which ones? Why not all? We know that some people are sexually aroused or oriented toward the opposite sex (heterosexual), the same sex (homosexual), or both sexes (bisexual). We also know that some people are sexually oriented towards infants, children and youths. Still others are sexually oriented towards sheep, cattle or dogs. There are cases on record of people having a sexual attraction to shoes. And some people are sexually aroused by rape, violence and murder. Although the campaign right now is to get homosexual orientation put across as a human rights issue, it is not clear whether or why these other orientations should not also receive the same protection, based on the same arguments.

Another issue is, how far will proposed legislation be enforced? Would a single mother with young children who had a basement suite to rent be forced to rent that suite to those who engage in sexual practices that offend her religious or moral views? Or would a school board be forced to hire individuals who engage in sexual practices that offend that community's commonly held moral standards?

Would Canadian Christian schools (Roman Catholic or Protestant) be required to permit homosexual activist groups to function on their campuses, as happened in the case of the

Catholic Georgetown University in the United States? Would Canadian Big Brothers and Big Sisters be forced to accept homosexuals and pair them up with "little brothers" and "little sisters," without informing the parents as was attempted in Minneapolis, Minnesota?

Must Canadian Christians, Jews, Muslims and Zoroastrians, whose deeply held *belief systems* declare that homosexual *behaviour* is immoral, be forced by alleged "human rights" laws to have their children taught the *belief systems* of the homosexual lobby or of other similar lobbies that may follow in its wake? Why should they be compelled to support with their taxes a public school system whose counsellors will refer their teenagers, if confused about their sexual identity, to gay and lesbian organizations for help?

These are proposals being prepared right now, if they are not already law in your jurisdiction.[3] If homosexual lobby groups are politically active and parent groups are politically inactive, we may reasonably expect laws of this kind to become general.

Legal "Gay" Marriages?

Some homosexual lobbyists want all the rights and benefits which are available to married couples to be available to themselves and their current partners. They argue that because they live together, prepare meals together and care for each other, they should be able to legally marry. But the lobby's argument is not only about "personal closeness" and "sharing". They are not trying to extend the definition of marriage to just any two housemates who help each other out. The premise behind the argument is that their sexual *behaviour* together constitutes a marriage. They want the fact that they masturbate or sodomize each other to be recognized as the basis for marriage.

In the Mossop case in Canada in 1993, it was argued that homosexuals should be considered a "family." Brian Mossop wanted to claim "family" bereavement days from work to attend the funeral of his male lover's father. Now, it may well be the case that the law should provide that all individuals may miss work to attend funerals important to them, irrespective of family relationship. But to argue from this individual right that any two people who share an apartment and engage in sexual acts are a family is ludicrous.

Homosexual lobbyists want more than to be defined as a "family". They want the right to take in foster or adoptive children as well. And, in pursuit of this goal, militant lesbians have become artificially inseminated or have had a "one night stand" with a man in order to bear children to be raised in a "homosexual family." This latter action demonstrates, as nothing else could, the profoundly unnatural basis of homosexual couplings.

It is worth recalling the history of relations between the Judeo-Christian approach to marriage and other points of view that existed in ancient times. The Judeo-Christian belief that it is the Lord's intention that sexual activity should be confined to a life-long monogamous heterosexual marriage challenged many sexual practices in the Graeco-Roman world. Adult homosexual practice and pedophilia were common, even though they were ridiculed and disapproved. It has been suggested that these practices reflected the low status of women in the society of the day.[4] Women were not generally considered companions for men, in the Genesis sense. For example, the classical Greek and Roman words for virtue (*arete* and *virtus*) both meant "male-ness." Not surprisingly, men found their meaningful relationships with other men or boys, and sometimes these were sexual relationships. Men were encouraged to seek sexual pleasure wherever they wished, with societal approval, as long as they did so "in moderation," and did not violate the rights of other men.

But when Christianity swept into the Mediterranean world, it brought with it a moral revolution that completely transformed sexual mores. Historian Lawrence Stone noted this remarkable shift as follows:

> Whatever the cause of this great moral mutation, which at the moment remains obscure, the result was a shift from a bi-sexual world divided between the penetrators and the penetrated, to one divided between reproductive hetero-sexuality and sterile homosexuality; from one of marriage as a relatively rare legal condition undertaken for purposes of property disposal and inheritance, to marriage as a normal condition of that great majority of mankind unable to live a life of total chastity; from one of ethically neutral bi-sexual promiscuity in marriage, to an ideal of male and female marital fidelity; from the moral acceptability of the use of slaves against their own wills as sexual playthings, to a new universal code of sexual behaviour no longer dependant upon the status of the parties involved. . . .[5]

It is surprising that Lawrence Stone finds the cause of the "great moral mutation" to be "obscure." The cause was quite clear: as Christianity spread, the Judeao-Christian understanding of the relationship between men and women (from Genesis 1 and 2) was replacing the Graeco-Roman pagan approach. The commands of God were being lived out in the growing Christian community. The three great biblical themes of marriage, the equality in creation of men and women, and the liberation of the poor, when faithfully embodied in the lives of Christians, transformed not only their families but also the society in which they lived. The second century *Letter to Diognetus* (5:1-14) put it this way:

> Christians cannot be distinguished from the rest of the human race by country or language or customs. They do not live in cities of their own; they do not use a peculiar form of speech; they do not follow an eccentric manner of life. This doctrine of theirs has not been discovered by the ingenuity or deep thought of inquisitive men, nor do they put forward a merely human teaching, as some peo-

> ple do. Yet, although they live in Greek and barbarian cities alike, as each man's lot has been cast, and follow the customs of the country in clothing and food and other matters of daily living, at the same time they give proof of the remarkable and admittedly extraordinary constitution of their own commonwealth. They have a share in everything as citizens, and endure everything as foreigners. Every foreign land is their fatherland, and yet for them every fatherland in a foreign land. They marry, like everyone else, and they beget children, but *they do not cast out their offspring. They share their board with each other, but not their marriage bed.* It is true that they are "in the flesh", but they do not live "according to the flesh". They busy themselves on earth, but their citizenship is in heaven. They obey the established laws, but in their own lives they go far beyond what the laws require. They love all men, and by all men are persecuted. They are unknown, and still they are condemned; they are put to death, and yet they are brought to life. They are poor, and yet they make many rich; they are completely destitute and yet they enjoy complete abundance. They are dishonoured, and in their very dishonour are glorified; they are defamed, and are vindicated. They are reviled, and yet they bless; what the soul is in the body, that Christians are in the world.[6]

Of course, one obvious result of the Christian way of life was larger families, which, in time, supplanted those groups who were unwilling to engage in relationships that involved procreation.

Will There Be a Return to a Non-Christian Basis for Law and Moral Values?

What the homosexual lobby groups want is nothing less than a return to the pre-Christian paganism of the Graeco-Roman world. They want sexual practices to be separated from moral restraint. In the name of "openness," "tolerance," "justice" and "love," they want doing whatever they want with whomever they want to have the same legal status in society as marriage. They want "sexual orientation" (sexual behaviour) to have the same sort of protection from adverse discrimination as racial origin. The momentum will certainly not stop with the current legislative proposals, whatever gay rights organizations may claim. We have already seen that the North American Man/Boy Love Association (NAMBLA) wants consensual sex permitted with children of any age in the name of children's rights. Is this really out of line with the goal of sexual liberation that is implicit in the Kinsey Report of 1948 or the kind of "value-free" sex education that is being promoted in many educational systems? Careful reflection will most likely lead to the conclusion that it is not.

The return to pre-Christian paganism is not only implicit in the "gay movement," it has been spelled out explicitly in a "gay manifesto for the 1990s" written by two Harvard graduates, Marshall Kirk and Hunter Madsen. Their 400-page book, *After The Ball*, concludes with a section entitled, "Gay Love Among the Pagans". They confess the emptiness, pathos and misery that the modern "gay lifestyle" brings to people's lives by the time they are thirty-five or forty. They are no longer attractive or sought after by younger homosexuals. What is their answer to this problem? It is to return to the "traditional gay family" of the time of Plato. They outline their proposal as follows:

> The ancient Greek model seems to have worked something like this. As an attractive boy – of, say, sixteen or so – passed through puberty (which, for nutritional reasons, occurred much later in those days than it does now) into youth, his boyish looks would attract the attention of an older, presumably more mature and established, man, – of say, thirty or so. The adult – following the youth about,

observing him at his work and play, and so forth – would form an estimation of whether the youth's character were as attractive as his body and face. If it were not so, it would be dishonorable to favour the youth with further attentions. If it were so, the adult would begin to "court" the youth, with conversation, presents, and the like, of whose meaning the youth would be readily aware. During this courtship, the youth would, in turn, form an estimation of the adult's character, as to honesty, integrity, maturity, courage, and the like – in short, the age-old virtues we all (should) admire. Should the adult not come up to snuff, the youth would refuse his presents and send him packing.

If, however, the youth found the adult as worthy as the adult found him, he might agree to become the beloved (*eromenos*) of his adult lover (*erastes*) – an alliance partaking equally of the qualities of father-son, teacher-student, and big brother-little brother relationships . . . with the superadded bond of explicitly sexual love. As with all relationships, that of the *erastes* and the *eromenos* entailed an understood exchange: the youth would share his beauty and enthusiasm, the adult his strength, security, and guidance – as well as more tangible assets, including training in arms, a position in the adult's business, and so forth. Both parties would benefit to an extent beyond mere genital relief. From the point of view of the community, as well, this arrangement discharged a natural need – for homosexual gratification – in a manner advantageous to public character and morality.

Similarly, it was understood that when the *eromenos* became a full-fledged man – and had absorbed all the (socially valuably) teaching that the *erastes* could impart – he would cease to be a lover, and would marry a woman and sire children. Neither his nor his former

> *erastes*' marriage, however, would end their friendship, nor prevent either one of them from forming a fresh alliance, in turn, with a younger male. . . and so on.
>
> Something like this, suitably updated (that is, without the wife and kids), is what we tentatively recommend as a new ideal for gay men – family structure of their own.[7]

Notice that their "modern" proposal has no role for women. And notice that since puberty is supposed to have meant that the "youth" in ancient times was 16, the "youth" today would have to be much younger. Hunter and Madsen are careful to state later in the book that they would "not advocate sex with minors," but what is a minor? Puberty, as they point out, is now arriving earlier in children's lives, often in the 10- to 12-year-old range. And modern societies, under the pressure of various lobbies, are lowering the age of consent. It is 14 years now in many jurisdictions and 12 years in the Netherlands.

William Gairdner points out that we are not far from this in North America. He writes:

> Unbelievably, radical homosexuals have become so influential and mainstream ever since about 1960, that by 1977 the U.S. Federal Commission on Civil Rights actually called (so far unsuccessfully) for a lowering of the age of consent for all sexual acts, from the current 14 for heterosexual and 18 for homosexual acts, to age 12 for both. Such a law would have given anyone the "right" to sexually use consenting children in any way they pleased without fear of parental interference. In other words, under such a law you could not legally prevent a 40-year-old from seducing your "consenting" 12-year-old son or daughter. In Holland today, the age of consent for homosexual sex is 12, as long as the parents do not formally object. Such laws, wherever they may arise in history, always represent a blatant retreat by the State from its traditional protections: of the family, of sound parental

> authority, of children from bad parents, of the sexual exclusivity of the family, and of normal procreational life.[8]

We have just read a rather "nice" proposal for consensual sex between men and youths made by Kirk and Madsen. It would sound nice when propounded by Harvard-trained intellectuals. But it is expounded more blatantly and passionately by homosexual Michael Swift in *Gay Community News*, February 15, 1987.

> We shall sodomize your sons. . . . We shall seduce them in your schools, in your dormitories, in your gymnasiums, in your locker rooms, in your sports arenas, in your seminaries, in your youth groups, in your movie theaters, bathrooms . . . wherever men are together. All laws banning homosexuality will be revoked. . . . Be careful when you speak of homosexuals because we are always among you. . . . the family unit . . . will be abolished. . . . All churches who condemn us will be closed. Our only Gods are handsome young men.[9]

It is not just a few individuals who want to extend "human rights" legislation to cover a wide range of sexual behaviours. Just as there are a large number of gay and lesbian rights groups, there are also a growing number of "bisexual rights" groups[10] and even "homosexual pedophile rights" groups, such as the NAMBLA. In addition, there is the Rene Guyon Society which urges "child-child and child-adult bisexuality starting at four, five or six" and has as its slogan, "Sex before eight, before it's too late".[11] These groups openly imitate the strategy and tactics of the homosexual rights groups. For example, the British Paedophile Information Exchange (PIE) argues that some people are just naturally pedophiles, just as some people are just naturally left-handed.

> Much of the medical profession in this country was content, until quite recently, to consider homosexuality an ill-

> ness. But as homosexuals have organized themselves to challenge this view, medical opinion itself has changed. Homosexuals are now widely regarded as ordinary, healthy people, a minority, but no more "ill" than the minority who are left-handed. There is no reason why paedophilia should not win similar acceptance.[12]

Once sexual behaviour is separated from morality, why not accept all forms of consensual sex? Will our politicians, courts, and educational systems which are currently blindly accepting the normality, healthiness, and acceptability of "sexual orientations" be able to draw a line to protect children? Right now it is conventional to do so; indeed, it is conventional to be horrified by pedophiles. But conventions change, especially when there is no clearly understood and rationally consistent moral principle underlying them.

Is It Possible for a Society to Shift Its Basic Understanding of Sexuality?

Is it possible for an entire society to shift its basic understanding of the relationship of male to female? Is it possible to move from societal approval of sex within the marital relationship of man and woman to societal approval of any sexual activity that two consenting individuals desire, regardless of sex or age? It is nothing less than such a shift that lay behind the "grand scheme" of Alfred Kinsey, the scheme which provided the basis for his sex research. Kinsey's view of sexual liberation has been summarized in the following three points.[13]

1. The normal expression of human sexuality is bisexuality. That this capacity is not realized in many people is because of "cultural restraints" and "societal inhibitions", which are assumed to be negative influences.
2. Sexual contact with adults would be a normal part of growing up for children in a less inhibited soci-

ety. This adult-child sexual relationship helps to socialize children and assists the development of full sexual potential in adulthood.

3. Promiscuity and diversity of sexual expression correlate with sexual health.

The largest recent study on homosexuality throughout history and in many cultures would lead one to believe that such a change is possible. David Greenberg's *The Construction of Homosexuality*[14] implies that the normative sexual relationships in any society are a matter of societal agreement. These arrangements are so varied in various cultures that you can only come to conclude that they reflect deep underlying *belief systems.*

Take, for example, the sexual practices among the Sambia of New Guinea.[15] In this tribe, the young boys are taken from their mothers at ages seven to ten to be initiated into the male cult. For ten to fifteen years they act as fellator, ingesting the semen of older males, and then as fellated or semen donor. This practice can continue even after marriage, but usually ends with the birth of children. The underlying *belief system* is that by ingesting semen the children are receiving manhood.

If our children were transported in infancy to be raised in such a society, Greenberg argues, then that is what they would do. He argues that this is not in any way a genetic or even a psychological matter.

> . . . In the absence of any evidence linking the peculiar sexual practices of Melanesia with genetic difference, it is reasonable to suppose that if a bunch of Melanesian infants were to be transported in infancy to the United States and adopted, few would seek out the pederastic relationships into which they are inducted in New Guinea, or take younger homosexual partners when they reached maturity. Similarly, American children raised in New Guinea would accommodate themselves to the Melanesian practices. Where social definitions of appro-

> priate and inappropriate behaviour are clear and consistent, with positive sanctions for conformity and negative ones for nonconformity, virtually everyone will conform irrespective of genetic inheritance and, to be considerable extent, irrespective of personal psychodynamics.[16]

You may not be surprised to learn that homosexual authors use the Sambia of New Guinea as an example of the "normality" of homosexual acts,[17] despite the fact that this is an example of temporary behavior.

Societies that are changing "human rights" definitions to give protection to "sexual orientations" are in fact giving special rights to sexual practices which the majority of North Americans consider to be unnatural, unhealthy and immoral. It is on the basis of deep *belief systems* that Jews, Christians, Zoroastrians, followers of Islam and the vast majority of humanity have rejected sexual perversions. If North American politicians and courts intend to enshrine the newer, neo-pagan *belief systems* of Alfred Kinsey and the decadent liberal humanism of the late 20th century in the area of human sexuality, there will be a number of predictable results.

The first result will be a further erosion of the traditional family, with nothing better to replace it. Government will be increasingly called upon to supply the traditional family's functions, at a time when government is not even in a position to easily pay for its own necessary functions.

The second result will be an increasing lack of respect for public institutions, such as legislatures and the courts. These institutions are already viewed with great scepticism by a large proportion of the population. If they take upon themselves the role of promoter and protecter of unhealthy sexual practices they will certainly lose even more credibility .

A further result will be the collapse of the public school system, as parents who want their children's education to reflect values based on their deeply held belief systems opt out into private systems. The children whose parents cannot afford private education or do not care to try will be the biggest losers.

Ultimately, the sexual experiment in Western society will fail. We may be seeing the beginning of this failure in the worldwide AIDS epidemic, which is nature's rebellion against unnatural and unhealthy sexual practices, both homosexual and heterosexual. And surely G.K. Chesterton was correct when he said of the family, "This triangle of truisms, of father, mother and child, cannot be destroyed; it can only destroy those civilizations which disregard it."

The sexual experiment may have a great deal more damage to do before it finally peters out, however. How much damage depends on whether its advocates or its opponents can muster the more effective political action in the coming decades. But it is not enough to oppose something. The question is, what would we put in its place? We will now turn to look at the biblical roots of the deep belief system that underlies the Christian view of male, female, sex and marriage.

Study Guide Questions

1. "If homosexual lobby groups are politically active and parent groups are politically inactive, we may reasonably expect laws and policies of this kind to become general." (laws and policies giving homosexual lobby groups access to teenage minors through the school system)

Do you know what is going on at your public school board in this area? If you discovered that such a policy was being debated or was already in place, would you do or say anything? Why or why not? If you would do or say something, what would it be?

2. " . . . to argue . . . that any two people who share an apartment and engage in sexual acts are a family is ludicrous." That is Don Faris's view. What is your view? What do you think should legally constitute a family?

3. "Every foreign land is their fatherland, and yet for them every fatherland is a foreign land." (second-century *Letter to Diognetus*, on Christians)

Would this description fit your life today? Or do you conform pretty much to the society around you? Discuss.

4. "Government will increasingly be called on to supply the traditional family's functions . . . "

To what extent can government supply the traditional family's functions? What about cases where the family structure has broken down? In your opinion, is government involvement in these areas a major milestone in social progress, a necessary evil or a big and costly mistake? Discuss. (If you think that government involvement is a big and costly mistake, what would you recommend instead?)

5. "Ultimately, the sexual experiment in Western society will fail." Apart from AIDS, is there any evidence for such a failure? Discuss.

So God created man in his own image, in the image of God He created him; male and female He created them.

Genesis 1:27

Therefore a man leaves his father and his mother and cleaves to his wife, and they become one flesh.

Genesis 2:24

Jesus answered, "Have you not read that He who made them from the beginning made them male and female?" and said, "For this reason a man shall leave his father and mother and be joined to his wife and the two shall become one."

Matthew 19:4

You shall not lie with a male as with a woman; it is an abomination.

Leviticus 18:22

For this reason God gave them up to dishonourable passions. Their women exchanged natural relations for unnatural, and the men likewise gave up natural relations with women and were consumed with passion for one another, men committing shameless acts with men and receiving in their own persons the due penalty for their error.

Romans 1:26-27

CHAPTER FOUR

What Does The Bible Say About Homosexual Practice?

Before we even begin to consider what the Bible says about homosexual practice, we must acknowledge what the Bible says generally about men and women and marriage. It is possible to go very far astray, and many people have gone very far astray, by looking only at a single text and ignoring the pattern of Biblical revelation.

There is, in fact, a clear and consistent pattern that runs throughout Scripture from the book of Genesis to the book of Revelation. This begins with Genesis 1, which teaches that human beings are created "in God's image – male and female". In the book of Genesis, humanity is explained as a *dimorphous* ("two-part") creation. That is, humanity is a single creation that exists in two *complementary* forms. These two forms complete each other. Neither women by themselves nor men by themselves are humanity. They belong together and must be considered together for any understanding of humanity as a whole.

The complementarity of male and female is such that, in sexual union, male and female become "one flesh." In other words, sexual union embodies the fact that humanity is a dimorphous creation. The union of man and woman is part of the goodness of creation, and is intended both for companionship and for procreation[1]. The joy which the union brings to men and women is gloriously celebrated in the Song of Solomon. The book of Revelation, seeking an image of the union of Christ and his people, celebrates it as the union of the bridegroom and the bride (Rev. 21:1, 9). Thus, the last book of the Bible returns to the subject of the first in order to find an image for the new heaven and earth.

Jesus clearly affirms the revelation of Genesis that men and women are created for faithfulness in marriage ("and the two shall become one").[2] The Apostle Paul affirms what both Jesus and the Old Testament Scriptures taught (I Cor. 6:9-11a; Eph. 5:3-7). But it is important to understand that all these texts, both those dealing with marriage and those dealing with homosexual practices, are *not* simply a list of rules for living or for condemnation of sin. They are part of the witness of the Bible about the nature of humanity itself.

This clear and consistent witness that runs throughout Scripture has a negative side as well. If God's will and intention is for faithfulness in marriage and celibacy in singleness (see Matthew 19:10-12), then there are sexual practices that are not in accord with God's will and intention because they violate the basic meaning and integrity of the sexual act. Adultery, incest, homosexual practice, and bestiality are all clearly condemned as not being consistent with God's will and intention for human sexuality. They are all equally, in New Testament terms, forms of immorality or sexual irregularity (*porneia*).

In neither the Old nor the New Testament is homosexual practice elevated above other sinful acts as being "more sinful", or the "greatest sin" or an "unforgivable sin". But, along with adultery, incest, bestiality, drunkenness, murder and greed, such a practice is considered to be sinful and unjust. Every reference to homosexual practice in the Old and New Testaments is a condemnation. Leviticus 18:22; Leviticus 20:13; Romans 1:26-27; I Corinthians 6:9; and I Timothy 1:10 all directly condemn homosexual acts. Genesis 19:5; Judges 19:22; II Peter 2:6-8; and Jude 7 condemn homosexual acts indirectly.[3]

Despite this, many liberal Christians have accepted the ideology behind the "gay lifestyle." Without reference to the Bible or to the way of life that Jews and Christians have lived for thousands of years based on its teachings, they have accepted the idea that there is no important difference between heterosexuality and homosexuality. How does this presupposition affect their interpretation of Scripture?

The majority of the very liberal committees appointed by some Protestant denominations to study the issue of homosexual ordination have shared two common failings:

First, they have failed to set the issue of homosexuality in the context of the biblical teaching on human sexuality in general, on which I have touched above. They have attempted to deal with isolated texts that speak of homosexual practice directly, without first examining the clear biblical teaching on human sexuality (Genesis 1-3), in the light of which these texts must be interpreted in order for their meaning to be grasped.

This practice of narrowly focusing on one passage allows them to assert, for instance, that Jesus had nothing to say about homosexual practice, as if that were a crucial piece of evidence that such practices are acceptable. Now, it is true that in the Gospels Jesus nowhere specifically mentions the subject of homosexual practice. But would Jesus have had to disapprove of every type of objectionable conduct explicitly in order for condemnation of it to have any authority? People who assert this point of view never want to abide by the consequences of their own argument generally; they are engaged in special pleading on one issue only. For example, Jesus did not specifically mention rape or slavery either, but you will not likely find that the same person who asserts that homosexual practice is acceptable because Jesus does not condemn it, would say the same about rape or slavery. Jesus specifically affirms his Father's *order of creation*, which I have touched on above (Matthew 19:6ff). It is this order of creation that is the key to understanding the Bible on sexual issues. The homosexual's attempt to construct a sexual union without the other (complementary) sex is, seen from that point of view, outside of God's will for creation.

The second error that such interpreters make is this: Having ignored the clear and consistent witness of Scripture to the union of man and woman in God's order of creation, as affirmed by Jesus, they claim to work within an ethic based on the principle of "love," which, according to them, overrides repeated condemnations of homosexual practice.

It is hard to know what to make of this ethic of "love." Although it is claimed to be derived from Scripture, it does not seem to have any boundaries or specific characteristics grounded in reality, let alone in Scripture. But then, anyone who seeks to build a community based on men involved with sodomy, and not on the union of men and women (as in Genesis) nor on Jesus' affirmation of celibacy (as in a religious community, for example; see Matthew 19:12) is stepping into a void, in which Scripture probably has little guidance to give anyway.

Is the Bible "unfair to women, homosexuals, and the poor"?

Another tack taken by those who want Christians to accept homosexual practices is to imply that women and homosexuals are both consistently condemned in Scripture.[4] The idea seems to be that if the Bible is wrong to condemn women, it is also wrong to condemn homosexual practices.

Does the Bible condemn women? It is certainly true that biblical interpretation for centuries has obscured the part women played in sacred history. And the Bible has been misused to keep women subordinated to men in the church. But responsible feminist scholars have helped liberate both women and men by demonstrating the equality implied by the order of creation which runs through both the Old and New Testaments.

What do the Scriptures say about women? At the very beginning of sacred history, as we have seen, is the affirmation of the equality inherent in the creation of male and female together in the image of God for mutual helpfulness and companionship (Gen. 1 and 2). But in Genesis 3, after the Fall, God predicts that men will dominate women as the result of human fallenness and sin (v16). As a result, we see that, despite the great band of heroines of the Old Testament, women are more and more segregated and subordinated in Israel until their status in the intertestamental period is equivalent to slavery. Yet Jesus the Messiah radically challenged the standards of his time by both his actions and words affirming women.[5]

In the early church, the role of a woman like Priscilla was obviously equal to that of her husband (Rom. 16:3-5; Phil. 4:1). And I Cor. 11:4 clearly states that women preached and prayed in the early church, severely limiting the meaning of the passage in I Cor. 14:34-35, which is often quoted to limit women's involvement in church life. And passages like I Cor.7:3-4 and Ephesians 5:21-31 stress the *mutual subordination* of husband and wife, despite the patriarchal cultural setting of the day. Paul could not have missed the radically liberating implication of his words, "There is neither Jew nor Greek, there is neither slave nor free, there is neither *male nor female*; for you are all one in Christ Jesus" (Gal. 3:28). This equality in Scripture is the solid biblical basis for Christian feminism and the ordination of women. In any event, the creation of humanity as both male and female means that no society could be whole, in a Biblical sense, if all the power and influence were held by one sex.

Similarly, though the poor and slaves were oppressed through most of biblical history, there is a clear and consistent message that runs through both the Old and New Testaments that God is on the side of the oppressed, is the protector of the oppressed, and that He brings judgment on oppressors. There are many passages dealing with the liberation of the oppressed (to name a few, Exodus [throughout], Isaiah 61, Luke 1, Luke 4, Matt. 25, Gal. 3, James).[6] This message of liberation for the poor is the solid biblical basis that was the foundation of the Christian movement for the emancipation of slaves. It continues to motivate Christians to struggle for the liberation of the poor throughout the world today.

But what about the claim that, because the Scriptures affirm that men and women are equal before God and that God is the liberator of the oppressed, homosexual practices are somehow "liberated" and affirmed? In the first place, the dignity of women and the liberation of the oppressed are based on the very character of God as revealed through his actions in creation, in the Exodus, and in the life, death and resurrection of Jesus Christ. They provide us with clear ethical principles that help us to live out God's will and intentions for His people. Though these themes and the underlying ethical principles are positive, they have negative implications for situations and conduct that lie outside the order of creation. Thus, genital sexual expression outside loving, faithful, committed (heterosexual) marriage is wrong. Subordination, exploitation and abuse of women is wrong. Oppression and degradation of the poor is wrong.

A faithful church is called to live out the holiness, justice and love of God revealed in God's acts as attested in Scripture. When the authority of Scripture is undercut, the only really objective basis for personal and social justice is undercut. The messages of Scripture about the dignity of women and the liberation of the poor and oppressed have nothing to do with, and would be inconsistent with, condoning forms of conduct that lie outside the order of creation.

Does "Love" Override Every Other Principle?

The homosexual lobby argues that there is a "love" principle that overrides the Scriptural condemnation of homosexual acts. They argue that "loving" homosexual acts should be acceptable to Christians. They claim that the references to love in the Scriptures support this argument. Thus, any acts that seem to the participants to be "loving" must be accepted and affirmed by Christians.

They are, in fact, arguing that there is an overarching theme of love that is in conflict with the principle of creation in the book of Genesis (man and woman as "one flesh"). The view proposed by these interpreters is clearly not the Biblical view. In the first place, in the Scriptures love is not an abstraction, nor is it a feeling. God is love, and God's love is made known to us through God's acts in history as revealed to his people through the Holy Spirit.

Love, as understood by the Scriptures, is not in conflict with justice or obedience. The Holy Spirit led God's people to witness to God's self-revelation in history in the Scriptures. Through these Scriptures the Holy Spirit continues to enlighten and enliven his people. Part of these Scriptures are laws and commandments. Indeed, there is a love *commandment* that runs through Scripture. (Lev. 19:18; Matt. 23:11-12; Luke 10:30-37; Mark 12:29-31; Rom. 13:9-10; Gal. 5:13-15; James 2:8-9). Jesus not only affirms this commandment to love our neighbour but extends it by commanding us to love our enemy. These commandments are not opposed to God's love or grace but are gracious gifts.

Jesus made it clear that He did not come to abolish the Law and the Prophets but to fulfil them. He did not lower the ethical demands of the Old Testament; He heightened them. Jesus also made it clear that if we love Him we will keep His commandments (John 14:15, 21). And He commanded us to love others as He loved us. He loved us so much that He gave His life for His enemies. It is that costly love which is the basis for all Christian ethics, including sexual ethics. Paul was surely right when in a discussion of sexual ethics, he summed up his argument by stating that "we are not our own, we are bought with a price" (I Cor.

6:19-20). Biblically speaking, love, justice and obedience are not in conflict. Our loving God makes his will and intentions known to his beloved children for our own good.

Problems arise when the biblical understanding of love, which is entirely consistent with God's commands for human faithfulness and obedience, is replaced with a culturally derived principle of "love" arising from concern with one's own needs and desires. Lesslie Newbigin states the problem clearly:

> . . . our society is – in its central thrust – governed by a false creed, namely, that human beings are made for self-fulfilment apart from God, for "happiness" on terms that they are free to decide for themselves and apart from any consideration of what may be the ends for which God created us.[7]

Of course, in practice, in such a culture "love" must consist simply of people's feelings and desires, and it is these that Christians are asked to affirm as somehow inherently right.

"Homosexual" Interpretations of Scripture

In order to weaken the force of the very clear condemnations of homosexual practice in the Scriptures, the homosexual lobby is forced to trivialize the Old Testament. For example, James Nelson argues that the reason homosexual acts were condemned in Leviticus is because of a "biological misunderstanding" that is allegedly present throughout the Bible.

> The prescientific mind (particularly the prescientific *male* mind) assumed that the man's semen contained the whole of nascent life. With no knowledge of eggs and ovulation, it was assumed that the woman provided only the incubating space. Hence, the deliberate and nonprocreative spilling of semen was equivalent to the deliberate destruction of human life.[8]

But is it true that homosexual acts were condemned simply because they were the "deliberate and nonprocreative spilling of semen"? Is it true that the Biblical view was that "semen contained the whole of nascent life"? Certainly, it was believed that the male contributed a "seed" to reproduction. But so did the female. And God was held to add something as well. Listen to the rabbinic comments in the Babylonian Talmud, Niddah 31a:

> Our Rabbis taught: There are three partners in man, the Holy One, blessed be He, his father and his mother. His father supplies the semen of the white substance out of which are formed the child's bones, sinews, nails, the brain in his head and the white in his eye; his mother supplies the semen of the red substance out of which is formed his skin, flesh, hair, blood and the black of his eye; and the Holy One, blessed be He, gives him the spirit and the breath, beauty of features, eyesight, the power of hearing and the ability to speak and to walk, understanding and discernment. When his time to depart from the world approaches, the Holy One, blessed be He, takes away his share and leaves the shares of his father and his mother with them.

Contrary to what you would expect if Nelson's argument has any substance, there is nowhere in Scripture a condemnation of intercourse with post-menstrual, infertile, or pregnant women, which would be a waste of semen if the only purpose of intercourse were to produce children. Indeed, quite the contrary; the rabbinic tradition held that sexual satisfaction was an obligation a husband owed his wife, even in situations where she could not possibly conceive, such as when she was already pregnant, for example. This is consistent with the teaching of Genesis that the sexes were made for companionship as well as fertility.[9] Nelson's argument that homosexual practice was condemned simply because it was a "spilling of semen" does not provide an adequate explanation for Leviticus 18:22.

What was the reason for the condemnation, then? In surrounding passages, adultery, incest, homosexual acts and bestiality are also condemned. It is clear that Israel's faith was that the "one flesh" union of men and women in marriage was God's will and intention, as clearly revealed in creation (Gen. 1-3) and reinforced in the Exodus Covenant.

Rather than being an obscure text, as some of these interpreters claim, Leviticus 18 (the whole chapter, including the prohibition of homosexual practices) is honoured in the Jewish faith as the basis for the "Holiness of the Home". It is one of the texts read every year on the most important festival, the Day of Atonement. It is seen by Jewish commentators as one of the reasons for the strength of the Jewish family. In other words, any sense of obscurity disappears when the text is read in the context of God's order of creation and his covenant with Israel as a whole.

It must be noted that both the new Roman Catholic and Common Lectionaries of Sunday Readings *exclude every text* that mentions homosexual behaviour, including Romans 1:26-27 and I Cor. 6:9-10. This means that generations of Christians in these churches will *never* hear these texts in the context of worship. Our Jewish friends may well ask what is the basis for "Holiness of the Home" in modern Christianity if it is not based on the guidance of Scripture!

Leviticus 17-26 (The Holiness Code) condemns equally incest, adultery, bestiality and homosexual behaviour. Most Christians would agree that these matters are as serious today as they were 4,000 years ago. But self-declared lesbian activist Virginia Mollenkott argues that if homosexual practice is condemned, so also should the other things condemned in the Holiness Code be condemned today. For example, there is a condemnation of eating meat with blood in it, wearing garments with two kinds of cloth, planting fields with two kinds of seed, or having intercourse with a menstruating woman. Her argument seems to be based on the premise that the Old Testament must be interpreted either with a simple-minded literalism or not at all. In fact, Mollenkott and others raise this argument only when it suits their purpose. They all gladly quote Leviticus 19:18 in regard to "loving your neighbour as yourself" but reject the very next verse (Lev. 19:19) about mixing cloth and seed. They are very capable of distinguishing between the *ethical* portions of Leviticus and the *cultic* ones (having to do with the details of religious observation important at the time), when it suits them.

Jesus did not reject the *ethical* teaching of the Holiness Code (Lev. 17-26) on the grounds that it was only *cultic*. Jesus himself affirmed the love commandment (Matt. 22:36-40; Lev. 19:18), the liberation of the poor (Luke 4:18-19; Lev. 25) and the union of man and woman in "one flesh," with its implied consistent condemnation of adultery, homosexual acts, incest and bestiality (Mark 10:1-10; Matt. 19:3-9; Lev. 18:20).

In contrast to the special pleading and proof-texting of those who cannot afford to see the whole pattern of the revelation in Scripture, most Christians would accept Biblical interpretation which attempts to:

1) understand the text of the Old Testament ethical teaching in its own proper context;
2) seek out the theological and ethical principles that underlie the specific Old Testament teaching;
3) examine how the New Testament reinforces or negates a specific Old Testament teaching, and the way the underlying theological and ethical principles are applied in the New Testament context.

Jesus, Paul and the New Testament church took the ethical teaching of the Old Testament with great seriousness. At the time of the Reformation, the Protestant reformers followed the principle of using Scripture to interpret Scripture. Two thousand years of Christian tradition have overwhelmingly affirmed the clear and consistent trajectory that runs through the Old and New Testaments of the one-flesh union of man and woman as God's intention for creation. It was this theme that was the context of the Old Testament texts which condemned incest, adultery, bestiality and homosexual behaviour.

Some scholars writing in support of the acceptance of homosexual practices attempt to wrestle with this problem by arguing that modern, loving, long-term homosexual practices between consenting adults were not known in Biblical times and therefore were not included in the condemnation of homosexual practice and should not be condemned today. Other scholars of the same persuasion contradict this approach by arguing that there definitely were such relationships in ancient times. Indeed, these authors claim that the Bible records the homosexual relationships of Jonathan and David,[10] Ruth and Naomi,[11] and Jesus and the favourite disciple.[12] And Episcopal Bishop John Spong even claims that the apostle Paul was a homosexual, and that that is why he condemned homosexual practice so severely. Leading homosexual authors argue that Jesus not only approved of pedophilia but healed the "boy" of the centurion at Capernaum (Matt. 8:5-13) and so restored him for the sexual enjoyment of the Roman officer.[13] Perhaps the best thing that can be said for these interpretations of Scripture is that they give some idea of how the Scriptures will be read when each passage is divorced from every other passage and from the central theme that runs throughout all the books of sacred Scripture.

Yet another tack sometimes taken by scholars seeking to gain acceptance for homosexual practices within the Christian community is to admit that the passages of Scripture which deal with homosexual acts do speak against them. But, they say, these passages were written before the modern understanding of homosexual "orientation" arose and are, therefore, dated and irrelevant. This is somewhat like arguing that because the Biblical condemnation of *drunkenness* was written prior to the modern understanding of "alcoholism," therefore, the condemnation is dated and irrelevant. Or, to put it another way, it is *all right* to be drunk, as long as you are an alcoholic.

As I said at the beginning of this chapter, if the fundamental assumptions of Scripture concerning God's creation of man and woman as a complementary whole are ignored, authors writing in support of a homosexual ideology can have a field day with the individual passages that refer to homosexual practices. Often, they try to show that these passages do not single out homosexual acts as the *only* sin or the *greatest* sin. Having set up this straw man in the first place, they then claim that it is a most unbiblical view to see homosexual practices as the only sin or the greatest of sins. Of course, all that any reasonable scholar would assert is that *homosexual acts are viewed negatively wherever they are discussed in Scripture.*

For example, the well-known story of Sodom and Gomorrah (Genesis 19:5) and the less well-known story of Gibeah (Judges 19:22) are thought by most scholars to refer to homosexual acts. This does not mean that the bad behaviour these chapters refer to consists *only* in homosexual acts. Certainly, other injustices, such as inhospitality and rape, are part of the story and of the condemnations incurred. But the argument made by some scholars that these passages do not even *mention* homosexual acts is so inventive as to be amusing. Their quibble centres around the Hebrew verb "to know", which can be used in the usual sense, "to be aware of", but also in the more specialized sense of "to have sexual intercourse with". (For example, the King James Bible uses the same idiom, permitted in [older] English, when we read, "And Adam *knew* his wife Eve; and she conceived, and bare Cain . . ." [Gen. 4,1].) These scholars argue that the Hebrew verb translated, "to know" most often does not have sexual connotations. Mollenkott, for example, suggests that when the men of Sodom wanted the strangers to be put outside Lot's door so that they might "know" them, they might simply have had "a desire to examine the strangers' credentials". Yet, within three verses in both stories, the same verb, "to know," is used of sexual relations with women where the meaning is quite plain and, presumably, no issue of examining credentials arises.

The argument that these Old Testament passages do not refer to homosexual practices goes back to Biblical scholar Sherwin Bailey in 1955. He also claimed that the interpretation that the men of Sodom and Gomorrah practised homosexual acts was rare in intertestamental and rabbinic literature. This claim has clearly been shown to be false by more recent scholarship.[14]

It is certain, also, that there was a clear and consistent hostility to homosexual acts in both Palestinian and Diaspora Judaism. This hostility was directed toward homosexual acts either with adults or children. While it is true that some elements of Graeco-Roman society accepted homosexual acts between men and boys, it is generally agreed that lifetime adult homosexuality was scorned as "unnatural."

The fact that adult homosexual acts were consistently condemned by Judaism and widely condemned in the Graeco-Roman world does not imply that they did not exist, but rather the opposite. They certainly did exist, and we have no reason to believe that, among their supporters, they were thought of as any less noble, tender, caring or long-term than such relationships in modern times. The fact is, such relationships were condemned in the Judeo-Christian Scriptures and tradition because, like adulterous relationships, they were outside the natural order of creation, no matter how noble, tender, caring or long-term they were thought to be.

The homosexual lobby also attempts to discredit the very clear condemnation of homosexual acts in the New Testament. Typical arguments revolve around the following ideas: That only homosexual prostitutes are condemned and not homosexual acts as such; or that homosexual acts are condemned only when committed by persons who are not "naturally" homosexual. Gay activist John Boswell attempted to advance arguments along these lines in his book, *Christianity, Social Tolerance, and Homosexuality*. His views are repeated without any critical examination by other writers as if they are generally accepted (e.g., J.J. McNeill, James Nelson, John Spong, Virginia Mollenkott). They are, in fact, not widely held to be convincing. For example, his suggestion that the Greek word translated "homosexuals" in the Revised Standard Version should read "male prostitutes" is not even accepted by as sympathetic a scholar as Robin Scroggs (let alone earlier work by Arndt and Gingrich, Sherwin Bailey, the overwhelming majority of commentaries and the recent work by David Wright).[15] Boswell's attempt to weaken the very clear meaning of the reference to homosexual practices in Romans 1 by saying that it applies only to persons who are not naturally homosexual is likewise promoted by the homosexual lobby, but is not convincing to the overwhelming majority of scholars.[16] Certainly New Testament scholar Richard B. Hays is correct when he criticizes Boswell's approach as a case of reading into the text things that are not there and could not have been there:

> . . . that Paul intends to condemn homosexual acts only when they are committed by persons who are constitutionally heterosexual is to introduce a distinction entirely foreign to Paul's thought world and then to insist that the distinction is fundamental to Paul's position. It is, in short, a textbook case of "eisegesis", the fallacy of reading one's own agenda into a text.[17]

Hays points out that not only does Scripture consistently condemn homosexual acts, but so does the Christian tradition of the early centuries.

> . . . every pertinent Christian text from the pre-Constantinian period (Romans, the Epistle of Barnabas, the testament of Naphtali, [if this is indeed a Christian text], the Apostolic Constitutions, Clement of Alexandria, Minucius Felix, etc.) adopts an unremittingly negative judgment on homosexual practice, and this tradition is emphatically carried forward by all major Christian writ-

> ers of the fourth and fifth centuries (Chrysostom, Ambrose, Augustine, Jerome, et al). A critical reading of Boswell's own discussion will confirm the point: he is unable to cite a single early Christian text which approves homosexual activity.[18]

Similarly, Robin Scroggs' argument that Paul condemns only pedophilia, and not adult homosexual practices, ignores the context of Paul's argument in Romans 1, which is God's will in creation for the one-flesh union of man and woman. Scroggs also overlooks the obvious Greek Old Testament (Septuagint) background (Lev. 18:20) of the words for homosexual activity in I Cor. 6:9 and I Tim. 1:9. David Wright points out that if Paul had wanted to narrow his meaning to pedophilia, he could have used the very specific Greek terms for those who engaged in this activity.[19]

Finally, the theme of the one-flesh union of man and woman as God's intention for creation is so clear and consistent in Scripture that, in desperation, many who seek to gain acceptance of homosexual practices are forced to simply dismiss the Bible as having a "heterosexual bias." For example, Joseph Fletcher (one of the popularizers of 1960s situation ethics) writes,

> The "revelation" and the "tradition" have alike been antihomosexual all along. To escape this ancient and malicious mind-set will mean that we have to drop the almost obsessive-compulsive addiction of typical theologizers to the Bible in Protestant circles and to tradition in Catholic circles.[20]

More than that, those who refer to the Scriptural condemnation of homosexual practice are branded as "literalists" and "legalists". In place of this "literalism" and "legalism" the homosexual lobby claims to have discovered some "principles" of "love" and "justice" that overrule both the general theme of the one-flesh union and the specific condemnations of homosexual behaviour contained in Scripture.

Amazingly, those of this persuasion who have not entirely abandoned Scripture will quote the Apostle Paul in regard to "love" (I Cor. 13) in support of their arguments when he was, in their view, incorrect and unloving in regard to homosexual practice (I Cor. 6, Rom. 1). So too, those who see homosexual practice as a form of "liberation" will happily quote Torah passages from Exodus and Leviticus (Jubilee references, Lev. 25) to establish the "justice" theme in order to override the "outdated" Torah condemnation of homosexual practice (in Lev. 18, 20; Gen. 19) Both types of apologists will quote Jesus about love and justice and ignore what He says affirming the Torah (Matthew 5:17-20) and His specific support of the union of men and women as God's will and intention (Mk. 10:1-10; Matt. 19:3-9). Others will suggest that all that Christians need to do is to follow Paul's advice to live by the Spirit (Gal. 5:22); yet they ignore his specific warning three verses earlier that sexual immorality, in which he clearly included homosexual acts (Romans 1; I Cor. 6; I Tim. 1), is one of the many works of the self-regarding flesh (Gal. 5:19).

"Thou shalt not judge" – What does it mean?

Having imported questionable principles of "love" and "justice" into Scripture, principles that are not defined by anything that appears in Scripture, the theologian writing in support of acceptance of homosexual practices then declares that what really matters are "loving relationships." So, if any behaviour is "loving", it is approved. What is loving? Liberal individualism dictates that only the individual can answer that. When it is pointed out that all sorts of sexual promiscuity may be prompted by such a definition of "love", the theologian will hastily add another principle: the "loving relationship" must be a "long-term" one. Support of "long-term, loving relationships" is intended to provide sufficient guidance for Christians.

Now, it is difficult to understand how a practice that is judged sinful in itself can be made righteous by a commitment to go on doing it with the same person for the rest of one's life. In any event, it is by no means the case that the addition of the qualification that a relationship be "long-term" is thought to apply only to homosexual practice. Indeed, the United Church of Canada *Report* concluded that these same principles apply to bisexual practice.[21] And homosexual lobbyist William Countryman concludes that bestiality is acceptable.[22] Christian ethicist James Nelson argues that Christians should be open to the possibility that adultery might be part of a viable Christian marriage.[23] Why would these principles not also apply to "long-term, loving" incest, "long-term, loving" pedophilia, or even "long-term, loving" group sex?

If this argument seems far-fetched, let us look at it in the human terms in which the arguments are often expressed. One very moving illustration concerns a minister being called to a hospital room where a woman is dying. Another woman cradled her friend's head in her arms, stroking her friend's hair. They had been long-term, loving homosexuals. Who could condemn this love, some ask, implying that this loving act somehow validates a wrong relationship.

If accepted, that line of argument could lead to other scenarios: another hospital room where an old man is dying; a younger man cradles his friend's head in his arms, stroking his hair. They had a long-term, loving, pedophilic relationship. A young woman is dying; an older man cradles her head in his arms. They had a long-term, loving, incestuous relationship. In yet another hospital room, a man is dying; a woman, not his wife, cradles his head in her arms, stroking his hair. They had a long-term, loving, adulterous relationship.

Now, quite obviously, the Christian pastor is not called to minister to the dying in order to condemn anybody but to hold out the message of salvation. So condemnation is not really an issue in a real life situation of this type. But in any event, the homosexual advocate's deliberate choice of a deathbed as the focus of the question about prior relationships is misleading, for *all* relationships are severed by death. Eternity, not future conduct in this life, is the prospect seen from the deathbed. What the pastor would say (to a pedophile for instance) on his deathbed would be a very different thing from what he would say to the same man in his study during the prime of life. And certainly, while it is good to see any person express compassion for a dying friend, how can this provide the basis for ethical judgments concerning prior sexual relationships?

If the homosexual apologists' interpretation of Scripture seems to most Christians to lead to some bizarre conclusions, that is only because it is severed from the whole and pursued with one end in view, the legitimization of something that Scripture cannot really legitimate. Also, in a well-intentioned attempt to avoid legalism (reducing everything to rules and prohibitions), some authors have gone all the way over to the other danger of antinomianism; that is, concluding that there are no moral principles or prohibitions, that anything considered "loving" goes. Those who do not agree that anything goes are considered to be *judgmental.* And texts of Scripture are sometimes cited as proof of the antinomian position.

Some antinomian interpreters defend homosexual practice by arguing that everyone has sexual fantasies or temptations. According to them, the Sermon on the Mount condemns sinful temptations as much as sinful actions. On this basis, it is hypocritical for any Christian to condemn anything that anyone else does, because we all are tempted to sin. Of course, the real question for a Christian is not "What do I want to condemn? but "What does God condemn?"

It is clear that both the Old and the New Testaments teach that temptations occur to everyone and are not in themselves sinful. The Sermon on the Mount does not teach that condemnation applies to temptations in the same way as to sinful acts. What is taught is that sinful *intentions* are as bad as sinful acts. Jesus himself was tempted, yet without sin (the temptations in Luke 4, Matthew 4). We are told that Jesus was tempted "in every respect as we are, only without sinning" (Heb. 4, 15).

Antinomian interpretation also focuses on Jesus and the woman caught in an adulterous act. The text, "You who are without sin, cast the first stone" is quoted. How often the story is left at that point, with the implication that no type of sexual conduct should be condemned! But that is not the end of the story. The story ends with Jesus' words to the woman, "Go and sin no more." Jesus was able to accept and love the sinner but reject the sin. Should we not try to do the same? Is it truly loving of us to take a position superior to Jesus' and approve whatever people do in the name of some abstract "principle" of love? Aren't we really doing what Dietrich Bonhoeffer warned us about in *The Cost of Discipleship*.[24] Aren't we proclaiming cheap grace? Grace as a principle? Grace without cost? Grace without a call to repentance? Grace without a call to obedience?

Homosexuality as a Justice Issue

One of the most commonly heard arguments is that homosexuals have been the victims of social injustice (for example, they were exterminated by the Nazis along with other types of people whom the Nazis considered inferior). Those who do not approve of homosexual practice today are said to continue the tradition of the Nazis. The argument shows little knowledge of the Nazis. Nazi leader Ernst Röhm and leaders of the officer corps of the Nazis Brownshirts were homosexuals, and Adolf Hitler personally defended their behaviour, saying that it was "a private matter". Hitler used these Brownshirts as his major terrorist group against socialists, communists, trade unionists and Jews – until the Brownshirts became a political threat to Hitler himself.[25] In practice, the Nazis never let a moral issue of any kind get in the way of their desire for power.

The assumption behind this false argument is that Christians should approve of or agree with whomever the Nazis oppressed. While Christians should support human and civil rights for all persons, including homosexuals, Jews, Communists, gypsies and Jehovah's Witnesses (all of whom were persecuted and killed by the Nazis), Christians are in no way required to agree with any of these people's beliefs or to consider their practices to be necessarily acceptable for Christians. Nazi persecution does not make homosexual practice right any more than it proves that Josef Stalin was really a nice man (as diehard Communists claim), or that Jehovah's Witnesses are correct in believing that blood transfusions are against God's will. It should be noted that Karl Barth, the Christian theologian who wrote the powerful Barmen Declaration of the German Confessing Church, which opposed the Nazis, also very clearly rejected homosexual practice as being opposed to the command of God the Creator.[26]

Homosexual practice is a justice issue, but not primarily in a civil sense. Biblically, whatever is in accordance with God's will and intention is "just" or "righteous." Hence, faithfulness in heterosexual marriage and celibacy in singleness are "righteous" and "just." Adultery, homosexual practice, incest, pedophilia and bestiality are "unjust" and "unrighteous," not because of adverse public opinion, but because they are opposed to God's will and intention for humanity.

They are "unjust" in that they are rebellious in relation to God. They are unjust in that they are less than God's will for human relationships. They are unjust in that they oppress the persons who engage in them. They are based on idolatry. That is, they are based on the idolatrous faith that "my body belongs to myself and I can do what I like with it". This presumption means that one puts oneself before God: "It is *my* will and intention that will rule my life." This unjust and sinful presumption breaks our relationship to God, to others, and to ourselves. When we live on the basis of this idolatrous faith in regard to any part of our lives, we are living in a situation of brokenness and oppression.

Truly then, homosexual practice is a justice issue. Jean Vanier, that gracious Christian who has done so much for the oppressed around the world, puts it this way:

> My fight for justice is a fight for the liberation of all human beings. I long for the rich to be liberated from the weight of their riches and their craving for more, in order to enter into the spirit of sharing. I long for alcoholic men and women to be liberated from their slavery; I long for men and women who thirst for power and domination without regard for the weak to discover true service. I also long for those who are imprisoned in homosexuality to find a free heart capable of loving someone of the other sex and becoming fruitful. I too have my *blockages*, and each day I must work and struggle towards a greater *liberation*. I believe that Jesus has come to lead men and women to liberty. The only condition for moving toward that liberation is to open our hearts to God, to know and accept our own poverty and fragility and to seek help.[27]

We shall examine in the next chapter some of the *blockages*, to the *real liberation* of homosexuals that have been created by recent revisions of language, theology and ethics.

Study Guide Questions

1. From your observations of yourself, your friends, your church, how do you think today's Christians view marriage? How well does that view fit with Scripture's teaching on marriage? Discuss.

2. How might a deeper understanding of the creation of humanity as a dimorphous ("two-part") whole help us understand women's rights issues? Or "men's rights" issues? What demands by militant groups could we support on the basis of this understanding? Are there demands that this understanding would not support or would greatly modify? Explain.

Can a society be healthy if one sex is overwhelmingly dominant? Discuss.

3. We have seen that a culturally derived principle of "love", based on one's own feelings and needs, can replace the Biblical understanding of love. Are there areas other than the homosexual issue where you can see this happening? Explain.

4. If you were to choose texts from both the Old and the New Testaments for a Christian series of readings on the Holiness of the Home, what texts would you choose? What should be the central themes? What other themes would you touch on?

. . . Present your bodies as a living sacrifice, holy and acceptable to God, which is your spiritual worship. Do not be conformed to this world *but be transformed by the renewal of your mind, that you may prove what is the will of God, what is good and acceptable and perfect.*

Romans 12:1-2

. . . Our struggle is not against enemies of blood and flesh, but against the rulers, against the authorities, against the cosmic powers of this present darkness. . . .

Ephesians 6:12

CHAPTER FIVE

All Cats Are Grey: Attempts to Revise Language, Theology and Ethics

Revision of Language

One of the reasons for the success of the homosexual ideology in North America is that the homosexual lobby has been able to control the debate by controlling the language. They have insisted that, rather than being described by the neutral term "homosexuals", they should be referred to as "gays." The neutral term "homosexuals" attempts to describe them by what they do, which they want to avoid.

To those not involved in the gay lifestyle, the term "gay" implies a positive, happy, fulfilling life. To those involved in the lifestyle, it is a term that celebrates their promiscuity and unhealthy practices.

In the early 1960s, homosexual lobbyists used the phrase "sexual preference." Their argument at that time was based on freedom of choice. They argued that some people liked chocolate ice cream while others preferred vanilla. Why should people be discriminated against because of their "preference"? The weakness in this argument was that it implied that people have a choice about the behaviour that they engage in. The homosexual activists discovered that people who knew anything about their behaviour had a great deal more sympathy for them if they believed that they had no choice about it. The homosexual groups could attach themselves to the civil rights bandwagon by identifying themselves with blacks, and to the human rights bandwagon by identifying themselves with women. So the politically correct term became "sexual orientation." This term, which implies an internal psychological state over which the individual has no control, is nonetheless ambiguous enough to cover sexual practices as well.

Perhaps the most useful and widely used term in the new language coined by homosexual lobby groups is "homophobia" or "homo hater". They label anyone who disagrees with their lifestyle or proposals as "homophobic" or "homo hater". They say that those who disagree with them hate or fear homosexuals. These "homophobic" people are guilty of supporting "heterosexism", which is the idea that heterosexual relationships are superior to homosexual ones. They apply these labels of "homophobic" or "heterosexist" to the Bible, the Apostle Paul, modern saints like Jean Vanier, and former homosexuals alike.

One is tempted to respond to their new language by creating an even newer language.[1] Homosexuals could be described as being "heterophobic" or suffering from "heterophobia", the fear or hatred of heterosexuals. Their unnatural, unhealthy and immoral practices could earn the expression "moral phobia," as they appear to hate or fear common-sense moral sexual behaviour, to the point of taking risks with their own survival. After all, the viruses responsible for sexually transmitted diseases are not influenced by changes in terminology. Whatever the "sexual orientations" that are going on in other people's heads, it is unnatural and unhealthy sexual *practices* that have been causing an epidemic of sexually transmitted diseases, including AIDS, among practising homosexuals. And the homosexual lobby's attack upon the traditional family of mother, father and children could suggest the term "family phobia." But playing with words does not change reality and we need to do more than play around with words in order to understand what is happening.

Revision of Theology Through Language

The revision of the language used to describe homosexuality is an attempt to change the public perception of reality by changing the language. Guided by the insights of sociology in understanding the "social construction of reality", homosexual lobbyists know that in using a new language they will, in fact, be creating a new understanding of reality among those who accept it. It is at this point that radical feminists and homosexual lobbyists have a common cause.

Radical feminist theologians, for example, are also interested in changing language. Many of them are not satisfied with inclusive language for human beings, for which there is biblical warrant. They also refuse to refer to God as Father, or Jesus as Lord, on the grounds that these words are patriarchal and hierarchical. Some refer to God (or even Christ) in female terms. Now, there is Biblical warrant to use *similes* that say that God or Jesus is *like* a loving mother, a mother eagle or mother hen; there are similes of this kind in the Scriptures. But the use of these similes in no way rules out the Biblical insight that only God can *name* God.[2] And God named himself Lord in the Old Testament. Jesus, the Son, named God as Father and told us to call Him Father. Of course, He also named the Holy Spirit.

The Biblical language does not mean that God the Father is male, in the sense in which a male human is male and not female. God is beyond the limits of human sexuality. He is neither male nor female in Himself. But He is personal, and in revealing Himself to His people, the personal terms that He Himself has chosen, to show what He is most like, are words like "Lord" and "Father." On the other hand, there is simply no Biblical warrant for naming God "Mother". And the use of the absurd name "Mother/Father God" simply projects a hermaphrodite god into the heavens. At any rate, it is certainly a denial of God's self-revelation. It lays the groundwork for a human claim to be able to name God whatever we want, and to construct any social understanding of reality we want.

This is where radical feminism works together with the social-political agenda of the homosexual lobby. We have seen that the homosexual lobby wants to deny the revealed biblical understanding of reality and to construct its own understanding by changing language. The current debate in the church uses unbiblical terms such as "homophobia" and "heterosexism". These are political terms that have nothing to do with the Judeo-Christian understanding of life or of creation. For example, anyone who disagrees with homosexual behaviour is labelled "homophobic." Even people who struggle to overcome their past inclination to homosexual practices are described as "homophobic." And the Scriptures themselves are said to be "homophobic" because they teach "heterosexism," that is, the superiority of the sexual union of male and female over homosexual practices.

What the homosexual rights movement wants is to have the church declare that homosexual and bisexual behaviour is as morally acceptable as the union of men and women in marriage. This is not the view of the Scriptures. Both Jesus and Paul confirm the foundational view of Genesis that God's intention for human sexuality is that a man and a woman should become "one flesh" in marriage. All forms of sexual behaviour apart from this are irregular and adulterous. In a very real sense, it is true, therefore, that the Scriptures are "heterosexist." They uphold the creation order of God, who is the author of nature and of humanity, and the pattern of heterosexual union is his pattern.

Accepting God's pattern as revealed in nature and in the sacred Scriptures is a matter of faith for the believing Christian (or Jew). If the faith changes, then a new language, which expresses this new faith, will construct a new social reality. One by-product is that if homosexual, bisexual, and other sexual orientations are approved by people who wish to consider themselves Christians, the accompanying practices will increase in our society.

What type of Christian theology is open to such changes? Certainly, a liberal theology that is closed to its biblical roots is open to finding any number of new messages to proclaim. Having abandoned its Christian basis, which sees the Lordship and authority of Jesus Christ as central, liberal theology has often found a new centre in the personality of the preacher. The gospel mediated by personality soon became the gospel *of* personality. And what if that personality is a warm, smiling, open, tolerant, accepting father/mother figure? Not a good father or mother, particularly, but an indulgent one, who wants us to be "happy" whatever the cost. The gospel of "acceptance" and "inclusivity" has captured many minds in liberal theology, leading not only to the acceptance of homosexual practice but even to the acceptance of self-proclaimed witches ("creation spirituality"). When applied to sexual ethics, this type of thinking argues, essentially, that all cats are grey in the night – and, presumably, morning never comes. The thought seems to be, "No one is perfect. It is the 'relationship' that counts."

The gospel according to some is not "repent, believe and obey", but, "accept yourself." A simple surrender to one's own selfishness and immaturity is the goal; the new life in Jesus Christ is a detour to be avoided. Surely Christian ethicist Philip Turner is correct in suggesting that these attempted revisions of Christian sexual ethics comes from denominations that do not ask much of their membership.[3] They see themselves as "meeting needs" rather than "making demands."

The pressure for change in this area comes particularly from clergy who have incorporated the new "ethics" into their pastoral care. Their consumer-oriented pastoral care consists of agreeing with, rather than challenging, the mind of the times.

And out of this pastoral care "experience," they seek to change the teaching of the church.

Revision of Ethics

Three types of attempts to revise Christian ethics are popular in liberal North American denominations at the moment: libertarianism, self-actualization, and personalism.

Libertarianism holds that there is no such thing as a specific sexual ethic; all human relationships should be governed by the same moral restraints.[4] People should not exploit or harm one another, but apart from that, they should feel free to choose whatever makes most sense to them. This "ethic" reflects the highly individualistic society of North America. Its idea of social relationships appears to be modeled on the "contract" of the business world.

Self-actualization has much in common with the libertarianism but its central criterion in human relationships is that they must contribute to "human growth and development." Many ethicists of this school would argue that adultery, group sex, bondage and homosexuality might all lead to personal growth and development.[5] Indeed, though some forms of sexual behaviour may not be approved, in general no form of sexual behaviour is wrong in itself. One might conceive of circumstances in which bestiality, incest, pedophilia or sado-masochism might lead to personal growth. Self-actualization ethics can easily shade into libertarian ethics. Indeed, both share the individualist and contractual assumptions of North American society in general.

Personalism is also highly individualistic, but attempts to overcome this by stressing that a person must always be viewed in relation to other persons. It argues that persons do have rights and duties in relation to one another. "Respect for persons" involves love, care, trust, openness and, to a point, fidelity in regard to both the motives and the results of our actions. James

Nelson, the most influential personalist, stresses the "appropriateness" of sexual behaviour to the nature of the relationship and the level of commitment. He can speak of marital relationships requiring permanence but not necessarily exclusivity. Secondary relationships, possibly including genital sex, are compatible with his definition of fidelity. Nelson holds that many types of "non-marital" sexual acts may reflect love, care, trust, openness and fidelity. He defines "sex" as a biologically based need directed not only toward procreation but also toward pleasure and the release of tension. "Sexuality" is a more inclusive term, covering not only the biologically based need but also all feeling, thought and action. In short, it is our self-understanding and way of being in the world.

Philip Turner astutely observes that Nelson treats the body as a container or instrument that persons, who have some sort of inner mental reality called sexuality, use to do or say things. To someone who believes that the body is just a container of some kind, sexual orientation is unimportant. The body which initially distinguishes us as male and female is secondary. What is important is that one "person" strives (by use of the body) to achieve unity with another "person." This concept of the body as a container for the "person" (the important part) is called "dualism." As a point of view, it is at odds with the understanding of the body found in the Bible. In Jewish and Christian thought, there is no separation between body and spirit; for all practical purposes, we are our bodies until we die.

Personalists like to use the analogy of sexual activity as conversation. Just because a man usually has "conversations" with his wife, is no reason why he cannot have "conversations" with other women, or men, as along as they are "appropriate." And what is wrong with "premarital conversations" or man-to-man or woman-to-woman "conversations"? Or what is wrong with "conversations" with children or "conversations" in a group? All of these "conversations" are supposed, of course, to occur in "personal" relationships of love, care, trust, openness and "fidelity."

Personalism has proven the most attractive of these three modern revisions of Christian sexual ethics. It masks its unbiblical individualism and dualism more effectively than libertarianism and self-actualization conceal their rapaciously egotistical basis. All three of these revisionist ethics replace the important biblical concept of a covenant with the modern commercial concept of a contract. The underlying assumption that they all make is that the world is a sexual shopping mall and that we can negotiate any sexual contracts we like with one another and put them in our shopping carts. There is no sense that, as Christians, we are related to God and to one another in a covenant, freely and graciously established by God to reflect the fundamental nature of humanity, and therefore not negotiable.

Homosexual Liberation Theologies

Some forms of *liberation* theology reject a biblical basis of revelation and opt for a Marxist basis instead.[6] But without a biblical basis, liberation theology becomes mere political opinion, and not a particularly popular political opinion at that. Even if its political agenda succeeded, liberation theology is doomed because its Marxist basis is oppressive and economically faulty, a fact that will win it few friends. And if its political agenda fails, at the cost of much suffering to the poor, it will be because, ultimately, all ideologies fail.

Some "feminist" forms of liberation theology reject the Catholic roots of Christian tradition in favour of highly selective Gnostic variations. Not surprisingly, some followers of these variations have completely abandoned Christian tradition and are now worshippers of the mother goddess. These women welcome homosexuality as an attack on what they see as the male-dominated "family." Rooted in the belief that human beings are one with the divine, some (such as Mollenkott) feel free to proclaim their own new ethical systems. Some even want to "democratize" the Christian faith by refusing to affirm that "Jesus Christ is Lord." Many have adopted "political lesbianism" as a form of protest against male domination.

Having dethroned God and rejected the Lordship of Christ, this type of feminist theologian believes that, in sexual matters, all we need is "love." But Biblical scholar Elizabeth Achtemeier has asked, what does love mean to these people? Her answer is, "For many feminists it is unqualified acceptance of any life-style. Thus Ruether has written liturgies brimming over with acceptance of extra-marital sex, of lesbian 'marriage', of any divorce or abortion; even of female narcissistic examination of their bodies and menstrual blood. Anything is acceptable if one has no standard of judgment. Yet, our Lord tells us that love is defined by His words and action. We love Him if we keep His commandments, and we are to love one another as He has loved us."[7]

Achtemeier reminds us of this. She then presses on to ask what *empowers* us to love:

> . . . once again the Bible replies, only the Spirit of Jesus Christ at work in us. Human beings are sinful and selfish creatures, who always look after their own interests first and who will sacrifice almost anyone to protect those interests. Yet the proclamation of the New Testament is that our Lord has overcome the power of that sin and that by his Spirit we can in fact be enabled to love one another in community as he first loved us. There are only two alternatives: Either we are slaves of sin, or we are slaves of a Lord of love; and by repudiating Christ's lordship, feminists have deprived themselves of that one Power who is able, against the very power of hell itself, to overcome society's divisions and deathly dominations.[8]

I hope that nothing that I have written here will be construed as an attack on the idea that the Gospel is a force for liberation. There is a proper Biblical basis for liberation theology. This basis was used by the many Christians who fought against the oppression of slavery, and by many today who fight the oppression of minority racial groups, women, children and the poor. A liberation theology rooted in Scripture is essential to the future of the church and the world. Scripture clearly says that God is on the side of the poor, and of children, women and oppressed racial groups. And anyone who wishes to serve God must be on that side too.

Liberation theology is properly applied to gaining civil rights for *all* individuals in a pluralistic society. All Christians should support such civil rights. But the support of civil rights does not imply that Christians must support the promotion of sexual perversions. Unfortunately, the liberal, sentimental approach claims that both "social justice" and "love" demand the approval of homosexual practices. This application of liberation theology to the issue of homosexual practice is unbiblical.

Similarly, I would like to make it clear that I am not attacking liberal theology in principle. A truly liberal theology, open to the past as well as to the present and the future, has much to offer. But no theology is free simply to ignore the Scriptures and the Christian tradition while claiming to represent them. Scripture clearly tells us that God's will and intention is for faithfulness in the union of men and women in marriage and for celibacy in singleness. Those who try to undercut the authority of Scripture in regard to sexual ethics have no business running to it for quotations in regard to all other forms of social justice, whenever they feel like it.

The *homosexual ideology* put forward by homosexual rights groups has no foundation in Scripture and no place in the Christian life. In fact, the homosexual ideology is directly contrary to the consistent teaching of both the Old and New Testaments. It also runs contrary to fact in its claims that people are "born homosexual," that all possible sexual orientations are natural and harmless, and that orientations cannot be changed.

A Call to Faithfulness and Obedience

The churches of North America need to recognize the unbiblical nature of the individualism, dualism and contractualism that underlies the homosexual ideology, currently trying to disguise itself as a new Christian paradigm. We need to hear the clear call to faithfulness sounded in the Barmen Declaration of the German Confessing Church during the Hitler era when the Nazis were demanding ideological control over the churches:

> Jesus Christ, as he is testified to us in the Holy Scripture, is the one Word of God, whom we are to hear, whom we are to trust and obey in life and in death. . . .
>
> We repudiate the false teaching that the church can and must recognize yet other happenings and powers, images and truths as divine revelation alongside this one Word of God, as a source of her preaching. . . .
>
> We repudiate the false teaching that there are areas of our life in which we belong not to Jesus Christ but another lord, areas in which we do not need justification and sanctification through him. . . .
>
> We repudiate the false teaching that the church can turn over the form of her message and ordinances at will or according to some dominant ideological and political convictions. . . .[9]

In a dramatic way, the Barmen Declaration highlighted the fact that the majority of the churches in Germany in 1934 had been captured by the dominant culture. Today, the church in North America is in danger of being captured by the dominant culture. At that time it was the Nazi ideology, which many Germans hoped would restore their country, even if they did not believe in it themselves. This time it is the more attractive, and therefore more dangerous, ideology of relativistic individualism. Individualist ideology can take either a conservative or a liberal form. In the conservative form, it generally concentrates on materialism; in the liberal form, it goes in for self-indulgence.

This ideology of individualism is examined in Robert Bellah's *Habits of the Heart.*

The danger of relativism to our ability to think clearly is discussed in the late Allan Bloom's *The Closing of the American Mind.* This ideology holds that all lifestyles are equally valid. With no basis for judgment or discrimination, "openness" and "tolerance" see all things the same. This makes possible a systematic irrationality. It is easy to see how the "homosexual ideology" can be part of the larger ideology of relativistic individualism. It is easy, also, to understand why social scientists who do not accept that premise, such as Charles Socarides, can object to the "normalization" of homosexuality as being "scientific unreason."

Reginald Bibby, in his recent study of religion in Canada, pointed out that, in Canada, religion tends to follow culture. The acceptance of the homosexual ideology by the liberal leadership of North American denominations is certainly an example of this tendency. But in contrast, the Barmen Declaration calls the church to be the church. It calls the church to be faithful to the one Word of God to whom it must be faithful, Jesus Christ as attested in the Scripture. To abandon our proper Biblical, theological base is to betray Christ and the world for which He died. It is, very specifically, to betray suffering homosexuals, who as we see in the next chapter, can be offered hope and healing for their sexual disorientation.

Study Guide Questions

1. Have you ever decided that you had no control over a certain aspect of your behaviour? Did you feel a sense of relief? At what price might this relief have been purchased?

2. "Only God can name God." What are some of the other names of God besides "Lord" and "Father" that we find in the Scriptures? What insight does each of the names you can recall give us about God? Using a concordance, try to locate the first place where the name is used, and some other places, and note the context.

3. Have you ever wanted to change your own name? What would you like your new name to be? What insight into your character does the new name give that your parents could not have known about? Look up Rev. 2:17. What kind of a new name do you suppose that the Lord will give to those who persevere?

4. "[Some churches] see themselves as 'meeting needs' rather than 'making demands.'" How would you rate your church when it comes to meeting needs? Making demands? Are there needs that any church must meet? Are there demands that it must make? Discuss.

5. "In Jewish and Christian thought, there is no separation between body and spirit; for all practical purposes, we are our bodies until we die." Does this assumption shed any light on the strong emphasis in Jewish and Christian thought on personal sexual morality? (See I Cor. 6:15-20.) Does it help you understand the doctrine of the resurrection of the body? (See I Cor. 15:35-57.)

Homosexuality is failure in functioning. . . . "which if carried to its extreme, would mean the death of the species. Beneath this obvious failure of function lies the agony, sorrow, tragedy, fear and guilt of a both unconscious and conscious nature which pervades the homosexual life".[1]

Charles W. Socarides, M. D.
Clinical Professor of Psychiatry,
Albert Einstein College of Medicine,
New York City

My fight for justice is a fight for the liberation of all human beings. I long for the rich to be liberated from the weight of their riches and their craving for more, in order to enter into the spirit of sharing. I long for alcoholic men and women to be liberated from their slavery; I long for men and women who thirst for power and domination without regard for the weak to discover true service. I also long for those who are imprisoned in homosexuality to find a free heart capable of loving someone of the other sex and becoming fruitful.[2]

Jean Vanier,
founder of L'Arche Communities
for the Mentally Handicapped.

CHAPTER SIX

Can Homosexual Orientation be Changed?

If a prevention was discovered for AIDS which had a 30 to 60 percent success rate, what would happen? Would this remedy be hidden? Would it be denied? Would it be attacked because it was not 100 percent effective? Surprisingly, something like this is actually happening.

If an individual is not already infected with AIDS, ceasing to live the "gay" lifestyle is the surest way to avoid contracting the deadly disease. But, far from being proposed as an option, changing one's orientation is the target of negative publicity among gay rights activists.

The defenders of homosexual practice deny that homosexual orientation can be changed, despite the fact that there are scores of cases of successful reorientation.[3] They also suggest that practising homosexuals can speak more objectively about homosexuality than can non-homosexuals or celibate or ex-homosexuals, and that therefore nobody should listen to people who say that they have changed their orientation, or that, if they have not changed their orientation, they are comfortable as celibates. This is a little like suggesting that only practising alcoholics can be objective about alcoholism. Naturally, as far as the homosexual rights activists are concerned, their cause is weakened when people decide to abandon the "gay" lifestyle, even if it is for the purpose of saving their lives or their mental health.

Before we discuss the ways out that are available to those who want them, it might be helpful to examine some insights about the psychology of homosexuality, in order to appreciate more fully the needs and challenges of the person who is attempting to exit this lifestyle.

Modern Psychological Insights about Homosexuality.

The first psychological theories concerning homosexuality were developed by Sigmund Freud.[4] He thought that the homosexually inclined person had overidentified with the parent of the opposite sex and then related in a conflicting way with the same-sex parent. He considered homosexuality to be a psychological disturbance relating back to these child-parent relationships, with some unknown biological aspects. Although he wrote that "the blighted germs of heterosexuality . . . are present in all homosexuals," he was not very successful in treatment nor very hopeful about it.

Several of Freud's disciples developed different understandings of the condition. Alfred Adler, who described the inferiority complex, saw homosexuality as arising from this condition. He observed that homosexually oriented persons invariably had inferiority feelings about their manliness or womanliness.

Yet another clinician with wide experience of psychosexual problems was Wilhelm Stekel. Like Adler, he minimized any supposed contribution from hereditary factors. He underlined the role of the same-sex parent relationship. He also noted what he called "psychic infantilism" and unhappiness in homosexuals.

Second and third generations of psychoanalysts built on these observations. E. Bergler noted what he called a "psychic masochism" – the homosexual drive containing within itself a self-tormenting need for rejection, "injustice" and suffering. Stekel's student Johan Arndt confirmed the earlier observations and synthesized them into the "self-pity principle." He observed this first in other types of neurosis and later recognized it in homosexuals. He was impressed by the resistance to change in adult neurotics who engaged in chronic infantile complaining. The treatment was to make the unconscious self-pity, "the inner complaining child", conscious, and thereby lose its power over the conscious mind.

Dutch psychotherapist Gerard van den Aardweg, while rejecting the existence of the Freudian unconscious, sees the most impressive characteristic of all neurotic persons, including homosexuals, to be their self-centredness, expressed in their addiction to self-pity. This "addiction to self-pity" is not something that is intentional or even conscious to the homosexual. And it does not necessarily affect the entire emotional life of the individual. It is an inner structure or mechanism of autonomous childhood/adolescent self-pity or complaining. Van den Aardweg has had success with an anti-complaining therapy, even to the extent of what he describes as a "radical" revision of sexual orientation.

Other researchers, such as Bieber, Horney, Sullivan, Eck, Socarides and Hatterer, have contributed to understanding in this field.

Another recent researcher whose insights have been found to be helpful in the treatment of the homosexual condition is Elizabeth Moberly.[5] She denies that there is any genetic or hormonal basis for a homosexual orientation, but emphasizes difficulties in the parent-child relationship, especially in the early years. For some reason, there is a deficit in the relationship with the same-sex parent. This deficit arises because of a trauma that has disrupted the normal attachment. The reparative urge to make up the deficit in love from the parent of the same sex is what lies behind the homosexual impulse. According to Moberly, the term *same-sex ambivalence* is superior to the usual term, homosexuality, because it describes a condition which exists prior to, and independent of, any sexual activity. More importantly, she argues that these same-sex love needs are natural and normal and that they *can* and *should* be met independently of any sexual activity. Moberly's insights have been found to be helpful with younger men and women. They feel that they understand themselves better when their attraction to others of their own sex is not seen as pathological. They can accept that their early hostile detachment from their same-sex parent is a problem, and can experience the repair of this deprivation of the past through same-sex celibate friendships.

Pastoral Support for Those Who Struggle with Homosexuality

One pitfall we must avoid in discussing homosexuality is "labelling". It is easy to forget that the condition which we describe as "being homosexual" or "same sex ambivalence" or "addictive self-pity neurosis" describes only a part of a total human being. We encounter the same problem when we label anyone. Is anyone only an "alcoholic" or "an adulterer" or "rich" or "poor"? Certainly not. There are many dimensions and many relationships in any person's life that are not seriously harmed by their areas of weakness and failure. Those who have homosexual tendencies in regard to their sex life, may be seen to have "a deficit" or "an immaturity" in that part of their life, while exhibiting great strengths and maturity in other parts of their personality. It is precisely this strength and maturity that is the basis for hope in treatment. This maturity can be the basis for the healing that can grow and spread through the whole personality.

The more understanding of the development of homosexuality that pastors and committed laity have, the better for their ministry in this area. Quite frequently, confused and anxious young people will approach caring adults with questions arising from homosexual fantasies or experiences. It is important to recognize that transient homosexual episodes may often occur during the confused adolescent stage of life. These occurrences do not mean that the person is a homosexual. The vast majority of these young people will pass on to a mature heterosexuality. But those who are homosexually inclined can be offered treatment with a very good probability of success at this early stage. For pastors or counsellors to tell such confused young people that they "are homosexual" or that "homosexuality is normal" and "cannot be treated" is misguided and could have tragic consequences. Pastors should become aware of helpful resources, of psychotherapists and self-help groups.[6] In addition to the growing number of Christian self-help groups, there are an increasing number of excellent written resources.[7]

The Response of Gay Rights Activists

It is interesting to note the response of authors such as John Spong and Virginia Mollenkott, who espouse a "pro-homosexual ideology", to insights into the causes of homosexual inclination. Both simply assert, without a shred of evidence, that homosexual orientation cannot be changed.

Mollenkott uses the argument that many famous men and women were homosexuals. She seems to be arguing, "Look at these famous people; if they were homosexual, it must be normal and healthy". Alas, even longer lists could be prepared of "famous people" who were alcoholics, pedophiles or manic-depressives. Fame has never been a guarantee of mental health, or even a very good argument for it.

Mollenkott also argues that, because a number of psychoanalytic theories have been developed to explain homosexuality, they must all be invalid. She seems to imply that if there were only one single theory, it would be more likely to be true. In fact, theories in medicine, and science generally, are usually developed to explain what has been observed. As a result, when a complex situation is being observed, different theories are developed to explain different aspects of what is observed. For example, light can be explained both as particles and as waves. Some might argue that this is contradictory, since light must be one or the other. But it is not contradictory; the two theories take into account two aspects of the same subject – light. Whatever light is, it behaves both like particles and like waves; therefore, neither theory is invalidated by the existence of the other theory. In the same way, a range of insights into homosexuality simply enrich our understanding and our ability to offer help. Barnhouse points out that psychotherapists have had success in the treatment of homosexuality using a wide variety of treatment modalities. Some approaches help some people, while other approaches help others. This fact by no means invalidates any approach.

Finally, Mollenkott, along with other authors espousing a pro-homosexual ideology, suggests that a study done by Evelyn Hooker in 1954 proves that homosexuals are not neurotic, and presumably, therefore, that there should be no problem for anybody living a "gay" lifestyle. Barnhouse, however, points out that the Rorschach test used by Hooker was never intended to identify neuroses.[8] Gerard van den Aardweg refutes Mollenkott's view simply by citing the many more recent studies which do use instruments designed to identify neurosis and do show significant differences between homosexual and heterosexual groups.[9]

4. The Cost of Trying to Make the "Gay" Lifestyle Seem "Normal"

Dr. Charles Socarides, who has spent a lifetime helping suffering homosexuals whom society scorned and ignored, is appalled by the personal and social cost that will result from the "normalization" of homosexuality. In the foreword to a recent book, *On the Origins and Treatment of Homosexuality*, he wrote that

> Dr. van den Aardweg's book is really a plea for help for the individual homosexual who has to cope with what an unfortunate childhood upbringing has so cruelly forced upon him. Homosexuals can only feel despair that psychology and psychiatry have forsaken them, were it not for volumes similar to Dr. van den Aardweg's.[10]

Dr. Socarides warns that:

> The psychological and psychiatric nonsense and social recklessness of "normalization" may well bring social and individual tragedy. There may well be a rise in homosexuality of the nonobligatory type at first, but ultimately profound gender-identity disturbances may increase and more true homosexual deviations will result as parents distort the maleness and femaleness of their infants and children.[11]

He is concerned that homosexuals themselves would be the first to suffer as, "homosexuals in therapy would develop resistance to therapy, retarding their progress, while others may be unwisely dissuaded from seeking appropriate help at necessary times. Suicides may well increase among persons with gender-identity confusion".[12] There would also be an increased lack of respect for psychiatry as "other medical specialists such as pediatricians and internists are becoming baffled by psychiatry and psychology's faulty reasoning in declaring this severe psychosexual disorder nothing but an 'alternative lifestyle' ".[13]

But perhaps most tragic of all would be the effect on young people. "Young men and women with relatively minor sexual fears will be led with equanimity by psychologists, psychiatrists, and non-medical counsellors into a self-despising pattern and lifestyle. Adolescents, nearly all of whom experience some degree of uncertainty as to sexual identity, will be discouraged from assuming that one form of gender identity is preferable to another. Those persons who already have a homosexual problem are discouraged from finding their way out of a self-destructive fantasy. . . ."[14] Surely Dr Socarides speaks for many when he writes that "anyone whose task is the alleviation of distress in people can only be saddened by the scientific unreason that has brought this to pass".[15]

Why are caring Christians moved to offer help to homosexually inclined persons? You need look no further than the lives of homosexual persons. The promiscuity, suicide, alcoholism and drug use among practising homosexuals are all signs of the great pain they bear. As is the case with alcoholics, some members of the homosexual community do not want help. They have reached a psychological equilibrium with who they think they are and what they think life is about. But other people do want help. Deep down they sense that they were intended to become "one flesh" with a partner of the opposite sex. They know that children and family are a natural part of most people's lives. If they are not called to celibacy, they yearn at a deep level for transformation from homosexual inclination to heterosexual inclination.

Yet, there are those who would argue that homosexual practice is a problem only because society has negative attitudes to practising homosexuals. Dr. Socarides states,

> There are some who argue that if homosexuality could achieve complete social acceptance, homosexuals would then be able to lead fulfilled and happy lives, free from any problems. In this light, psychiatrists who regard homosexuality as other than normal are attacked as tools of the antihomosexual establishment and become targets of abuse by homosexual organizations, the homosexual press, and even homosexual psychiatrists. We can only agree that the social rejection and discrimination that homosexuals suffer is unjustified.[16]

But Dr. Socarides' conclusion, based on many years of treating homosexual persons, is that

> If discrimination against homosexuals stopped tomorrow,

> as indeed it should, it still would not relieve their conflicts, anxiety, and susceptibility to frequent breakdown and depression. Society as a whole does not produce the homosexual condition, nor can it mitigate the psychological pain inherent in it. The etiology lies much earlier in life, and the anxiety, depression, and conflict stem primarily from intrapsychic conflicts, with only a portion derived from the shame and guilt arising from societal attitudes.[17]

Success in Changing Homosexual Orientation

The good news that caring Christians can offer is that help is possible. Scores of persons of homosexual orientation have been helped to achieve heterosexual orientation. Writing in the prestigious *American Handbook of Psychiatry*, Dr. Socarides states,

> To assume that homosexuality is experientially derived means that once the anxiety which originally caused the inhibition of development and the later appearance of homosexuality is removed through suitable psychological measures, the attainment of heterosexuality and heterosexual object love is possible. This has been verified in approximately *one third to one-half of all such patients* who were motivated to undergo depth therapy and to seek change.[18]

A highly respected history of psychiatry reported similar results. "The fact that *one fourth to one half* of all homosexuals who seek psychotherapeutic treatment can effect a reversal of their sexual interests attests that at least in these cases early psychogenic influences were most important in the development of the condition."[19] Ruth Barnhouse summarized the situation as she saw it in 1977 by writing, "Approximately *thirty percent* of male homosexuals who came to psychotherapy for *any reason* (not just for help with their sexual preference) can be converted to the heterosexual adaptation".[20] A 1984 report stated that

Masters and Johnson had achieved a 79.9 percent success rate which had remained at 71.6 percent after five years.[21] In his classic survey of the subject, Arno Karlen reported that successful change in sexual orientation had been reported in the 1950s by Drs. Allen, Bieber, Bychowski, Caprio, Coates, Ellis, Glover, Hadfield, Lorand, Poe, Rosen and Rubinstein. In the 1960s, similar change rates were reported by Drs. Cappon, Hadden, Hatterer, Lief and Socarides. Karlen summarized his finding by writing, "I have heard many clinical psychologists say they take for granted that they will get *complete change in a third* of their sexually deviant patients and *partial change in another third*."[22]

With such widely reported success in the treatment of homosexual inclination, Arno Karlen wondered why other therapists were so sceptical of these reports. So he asked Dr. Samuel Hadden this question: "Since you and so many others claim solid rates of cure and improvement, why is there still so much therapeutic pessimism?" Dr. Hadden's answer is interesting:

> Two reasons. One is that nobody likes to make a monkey out of his pop. Freud was our intellectual father, and he was very pessimistic about curing homosexuals. It took a long time for his children to say that he was wrong. What's more, the average therapist is often hostile to homosexuals, just like other people in this society. If you question him closely, he'll admit it. I've had psychiatrists come up to me at meetings and say, "I have a g--damn homosexual on my hands. Will you take him?" A g--damn homosexual! And you just can't hide from a patient that you basically don't like him and don't enjoy treating his problem. Many doctors tell homosexuals, "I don't think that I or anyone can do anything for you." They're expressing not only traditional pessimism but, in many cases, personal dislike.[23]

While traditional pessimism and homophobia are two reasons why successful treatment is denied, an increasingly common reason is the ideology of homosexual rights activists who frown on any defections from what they see as a political movement. Dr. Judd Marmor wrote,

> The myth that homosexuality is untreatable still has wide currency among the public at large and among homosexuals themselves. This view is often linked to the assumption that homosexuality is constitutionally or genetically determined. This conviction of untreatability also serves an ego-defensive purpose for many homosexuals. As the understanding of the adaptive nature of most homosexual behaviour has become widespread, however, there has evolved a greater therapeutic optimism about the possibilities for change, and progressively more hopeful results are being reported.[24]

The rejection of reality involved in denying that homosexual orientation is a treatable condition is so immense as to make one wonder why the pro-homosexual lobby is so insistent. It is almost as if its entire ideology would crumble if this cornerstone is removed. Is this the clay feet of the idol? Apparently so, for as psychologist Kurt Konietko observed, "The existence of one cured homosexual changes the nature of the condition in the homosexual's eyes. It challenges them. So they try to deny it".[25]

Three conditions are necessary for homosexually inclined persons to receive help from a caring church.

1. Those who offer the help must believe that help is possible.
2. Those who seek the help must believe that help is possible.
3. Those who seek the help must truly want to be helped.

If the church accepts the homosexual ideology that homosexuals are born that way and cannot be helped, it will *not be able to help* suffering homosexuals. Furthermore, if the church accepts the homosexual ideology, it will discourage suffering homosexuals from believing that *help is possible.*

Suffering homosexuals who want help will be forced to turn to other churches, other religions, or to secular psychotherapists who have not been captured by the homosexual ideology. By abandoning its Biblical faith that God's will and intention for humanity is the heterosexual "one-flesh" relationship that Jesus pointed to as the gracious will of His Father (Mk. 10, Matt. 19), the church will at the same time abandon suffering homosexuals. Jesus said He came to help those who wanted help, not those who do not want it. The church should be a place that offers help to those who want it. In addition to the helpful insights gained from psychology, the church should be equipped with the Gospel of the transforming power of Jesus Christ. If the church trades this Gospel for the politically self-serving ideology that homosexuals are born that way and cannot be helped, it will offer suffering homosexuals stones when they are asking for bread.

Three Difficult Options for Christians

Though social scientists may argue whether or not, or to what degree, some homosexuals are responsible for their homosexual inclination, all homosexuals are responsible for what they do. Everyone must make choices in life. For Christians who find themselves with a homosexual orientation, these choices must be made in the light of God's truth and God's love.

Persons with a homosexual orientation face three very difficult options. They can seek to change their orientation, to control it (celibacy) or to practise it. Quaker theologian Richard Foster wrestles with these three options with great compassion in his book, *Money, Sex and Power*[26]. His discussion of these options is based on the clear understanding that the larger Biblical context is that the union of man and woman is the norm for humanity. God created humanity "male and female" with the intent that they should become "one flesh". The idea that homosexuality is a special form of normal sexuality is unthinkable from a Biblical perspective.

From this Biblical perspective, the first option for a homosexually inclined person is to seek to change sexual orientation. That this is possible for some persons is a demonstrated fact. Those who are working for a change in their sexual orientation should receive the prayerful support and love of the Christian community. Their way is not easy and they need Christian friends who will stand by them in times of frustration, discouragement and failure. Our prayer must be that the life-changing power of God may help them in their situation. And when this happens, we can rejoice with those who rejoice.

Foster points out, however, that we must also be prepared to weep with those who weep. There are those who have cried out to God and seem to have received no help. Those who work with them have done everything they can and everything seems to have failed. What then can be done?

The second option is to choose to control the homosexual inclination. Through the centuries many persons faced with the homosexual condition have chosen celibacy. In an age which scorns celibacy, this will be a difficult choice. Those individuals who choose celibacy deserve the greatest respect, support and encouragement from the Christian community.

The third option for those of homosexual orientation is to practice homosexuality. Foster makes it clear that this third option is not equal to the first two. Homosexual practice is sinful. But that is not the end of the matter.

> We live in a catastrophically fallen world, and sin's distortions can at times entangle us in tragic ways. Human strength may not always permit the ideal. We are finite: there are limits to our knowledge and power. Of course, we hope for God's power to come; we pray for it to come; we expect it to come. When it does, it is a wonderful occasion for doxology. But there are other times of

> frustration, discouragement, and failure, and when those times come, we must manage as best we can.[27]

Richard Foster is clear that the church cannot give permission to practise homosexuality to those who feel unable to change their orientation or to embrace celibacy. But he says that if such a tragic moral choice is made, the most moral context possible should be maintained.

> A person continues to have moral responsibilities even when driven to engage in an activity that is less than the best. If we cannot condone the choice of homosexual practice, neither can we cut off the person who has made the choice. No, we stand with the person always ready to help, always ready to pick up the pieces if things fall apart, always ready to bring God's acceptance and forgiveness.[28]

It is certain that help is available for suffering homosexuals. What is not certain is whether Christian churches have sufficient honesty, faith and love to minister to these persons for whom Christ died. What is not certain is whether suffering homosexuals who are struggling to find sexual healing and wholeness in the church will be welcomed.

In the last chapter, we will look at what churches can do and are doing to make these things more possible.

Study Guide Questions

1. "One pitfall we must avoid in discussing homosexuality is 'labelling.' " Have you ever been labelled? What effect did that have on your self-esteem? On your ability to deal with problems? Have you caught yourself labelling others?

2. Can "labelling" ever be used positively? For example, Jesus called Peter "the rock." What effect might this have had on him?

3. Have you ever been told that you "shouldn't be concerned" about an area of your life where you were not living up to your capabilities or meeting your goals? What effect did it have on you? What would you tell someone else in a similar situation?

4. Are you ever told that something "must be okay" because "famous" or "successful" people do it? What do you think that Jesus would say in reply?

5. "Deep down they sense that they were intended to become 'one flesh' with a partner of the opposite sex." Many Christians have had to accept a life of celibacy to which they did not particularly feel "called," but circumstances have made it the only morally sound choice. If you are one of those, what experiences and insights have helped you? Are there attitudes or circumstances that you encounter which have made your life more difficult? (If you are not in this position, ask someone who is.)

And he arose and came to his father. But while he was yet at a distance, his father saw him and had compassion, and ran and embraced him and kissed him. And the son said to him, "Father I have sinned against heaven and before you; I am no longer worthy to be called your son". But the father said to his servants, "Bring quickly the best robe, and put it on him, and put a ring on his hand, and shoes on his feet; and bring the fatted calf and kill it, and let us eat and make merry; for this my son was dead, and is alive again; he was lost, and is found."

Luke 15:20-24

And the Pharisees and their scribes murmured against his disciples, saying, "Why do you eat and drink with tax collectors and sinners?" And Jesus answered them, "Those who are well have no need of a physician, but those who are sick; I have not come to call the righteous, but sinners to repentance."

Luke 5:30-32

CHAPTER SEVEN

Are Homosexuals Welcome in the Church?

Are homosexual people welcome in the church?
Are alcoholic people welcome in the church?
Are adulterous people welcome in the church?
Are greedy people welcome in the church?

They certainly should be. Everyone is a person for whom Christ died.

But I have been told by many ex-gays that they have had great difficulty finding a supportive congregation in which they can feel at home. There are times in their struggle for sexual reorientation that can be extremely difficult. Just as Alcoholics Anonymous members can have slips, so can ex-gays. Yet I know several ex-gays who have had slips only to meet with rejection from fellow Christians.

Loving discipline is something that we all need. By contrast, rejection is destructive, and it raises questions about the real commitments of those who reject. How many Christian congregations are really the warm, supportive, healing communities that they are supposed to be? How many congregations *really* face the fact that *all* of their members are helpless sinners, enemies of God (Romans 5:10) who have been saved entirely by His grace? How many of our congregations care enough about homosexuals to actively support a ministry to suffering homosexuals? The fact is that very few Christian congregations have reached out to people struggling with homosexual inclinations. Perhaps one of the reasons for the rise of the homosexual movement was this failure on the part of the church.

Not all the problems that former homosexuals face are caused by intolerant people, however. Another serious problem ex-gays face is the too-tolerant attitude. Some denominations or congregations, in the name of tolerance and love, condone or approve of homosexual behaviour. Former homosexuals have told me that they simply had to leave such groups. Some have gone to ministers for help during a rough patch only to be told that they "have no problem." While in the very midst of a struggle over a relapse, they are told that it is "okay" to relapse and that it is the "homophobic society" that is wrong. The life-and-death struggle these people face is certainly not helped by this "cheap grace". They are aware that sexual orientation is, at its deepest level, a matter of faith. Our deepest faith convictions about God's intention for human sexuality are the foundation for our sexual behaviour. So-called Christian groups that openly or secretly condone sexual sin cannot help in the healing process of those who long to be free of it.

Because all sinners (that is to say, all people) are welcome in the church, does that mean that the church must approve of everything they do? Of course not!

Homosexual acts are not the "worst possible sin." But homosexual acts are *unjust* in the same way as, for example, adultery, drunkenness and greed. As Christians, we call them unjust because they are contrary to God's revealed will for his creation, and are therefore not the behaviour of the "just," that is, those who have been justified in Christ. Rather, they all arise from – and result in – oppression, specifically, the oppression of sin. They are oppressive for those who do them, oppressive of their victims (consenting or not), and oppressive for society at large.

Our Common Need for Repentance

It is important that all Christians understand that we are all implicated in the circumstances that cause some people to have sexual orientations that are less than God's gracious will for them and for us all. We are all born into imperfect families, families that participate in an imperfect society, where *corporate sin* is at work.

The term *corporate sin* does not mean specifically sin by corporations – although that is certainly a good example of this type of sin at work. Corporate sin is the sin in which we all share, to a greater or lesser extent, depending on the degree of our power to change a situation. Environmental pollution, slums and unsafe workplaces are examples of corporate sin. Most people in a society contribute a little bit to the ultimate evil in each of these cases, if only by lack of concern or refusal to know. That is why the search that some people engage in for scapegoats (e.g., communists, big business, foreigners or some other group) is misguided; we are all responsible to some degree for these evils.

Families are also involved in corporate sin. Human sin, both corporate and personal, deeply affects all aspects of our development as human beings. This sin influences the processes whereby all of us are formed in our sexual identity. The result is that none of us, heterosexual or homosexual, perfectly fulfil God's will and intention for our sexuality. As Richard Lovelace comments, "We did not consciously choose to have the deviant sexual orientation which drives us toward fornication, adultery or homosexual practice. But we are confronted with the choice whether or not to act out our orientation and fulfil our natural desires, or whether instead to seek the control and transforming power of the spirit of Christ to restrain and re-orient our desires and our behaviour".[1]

All human beings sin and fall short of the glory of God. Therefore, none of us is immune to being unjust and oppressive towards others. However, God does not reject us on that account; God loves us sinners, even though He certainly does not love our sin. He has made a way for us to come back to Him to be healed and restored, through His Son, Jesus Christ. Because we are all equally sinners, we are all equally called to repent, turn away from sin, and turn towards Jesus Christ, whom we receive by repentance and faith.

Whether the sin by which we are oppressed (and oppress others) is adultery, homosexual practice, drunkenness, greed, pride or laziness, we are called upon to repent, to turn away from our sin, and to turn to Jesus Christ. The church, which He founded as His community, is a hospital for sinners, not a sanctuary for an endangered spiritual elite. But it *is* a hospital. In other words, those of us who have chosen to be there must accept that we all need healing.

Jesus did not say to the adulterous woman, "Go and carry on"; He said, "Go and sin no more." In the same way, we are all called to a costly obedience to Christ. If the Bible describes homosexual acts as sinful and unjust, it is not "loving" or just to "liberate" people by telling them that they have no problem and no need for repentance. That is what Bonhoeffer called "cheap grace." It is a crude imitation of what the church is supposed to be providing, which is *costly grace*, grace won at the cost of Christ's own sacrifice. Cheap grace is easy enough to dispense, but it brings no healing. Costly grace is difficult to dispense but, being the genuine article, it heals.

Some people will point to the fact that a popular minister who is a practising homosexual seems also to be a "caring individual" and ask, "Does *he* really need healing?" Yes, he does. Why should congregations accept ministers who are unrepentant practising alcoholics, or unrepentant practising adulterers, or unrepentant practising homosexuals? It is true that there are ministers with the above problems who demonstrate graces of sensitivity, intelligence and caring in other areas of their lives. But they have no right to use the fact that they may possess these other graces to claim that God has granted them a special exemption from the need for repentance in the areas of brokenness and sin in their lives. Still less should they be telling others that they too can dispense with trying to heal these broken areas of their own lives.

All church members, and ministers, are sinners. But we are all called upon to be repentant sinners. No matter what graces we may demonstrate in some areas of our life, we are all called upon to repent of sins remaining in other parts of our lives.

Welcoming Sinners

Truly welcoming homosexuals or alcoholics or adulterers into the church *means* offering them help. Many years ago the Methodist evangelist William Gowland wrote, "It might be more sinful to pass a pious resolution about prostitution and then retreat from the costly task of seeking to bring the prostitute to God, than to be a prostitute."[2] The church today is faced with a situation where it might be more sinful to pass pious resolutions *for or against* homosexual practice, and then retreat from the costly task of seeking to bring homosexuals to God, than to be a practising homosexual.

But a church cannot minister to homosexually inclined persons when some members of the congregation behave towards them with hatred and fear. "Homophobic" Christians need healing and love. It is often overlooked that these Christians are, in many cases, reacting from painful childhood or adolescent experiences of homosexual molestation or seduction. Or they may be reacting to their own problems of inadequate formation of sexual identity. Sometimes they are reacting to guilt from their own experience of transient adolescent homosexual episodes. In any case, the church must see that it has a great responsibility to minister to those who have developed an irrational fear or hatred of homosexuals, or of any other group. Such hatred or fear is in itself not only sinful but debilitating. How can a church minister to alcoholics if it fears or hates them? How can a church minister to prostitutes if it fears or hates them? How can a church minister to homosexuals if it fears or hates them? The church must establish, as a priority, a ministry of love and healing to "homophobic" members.

But it must be clarified that "homophobia" is the irrational fear or hatred of homosexual *persons*. It is not irrational to abhor *acts* contrary to God's revealed and gracious will for humanity. We should expect Christians to have such feelings about acts such as rape, incest, adultery, bestiality and homosexual practice. But feelings about these acts should not be transferred to the persons committing them. We cannot minister to persons who commit these, or any other sinful acts, if we cannot separate the persons from their acts. After all, it has pleased God to love *us* despite our actions, and this is the only Gospel that we have to proclaim to others.

We believe that it is God's will and intention that we proclaim God's love to hurting people, "homophobics" and homosexuals alike. On this basis, the church is called to undertake a serious ministry to homosexuals. We know that God loves homosexuals as his beloved children. How then do we minister to them? One thing that churches can certainly do is provide a climate of encouragement for those homosexuals who are motivated to try reorientation. These individuals typically receive criticism and discouragement from other practising homosexuals, who view them as "defectors." Probably they will therefore lose their accustomed social group and be quite lonely. Recent developments in the understanding and treatment of the homosexual condition (e.g., Moberly, van den Aardweg) have produced success rates for reorientation in the thirty to sixty percent range. This is higher than the success rate in the treatment of alcoholism and many other deeply rooted disorders. A combination of these forms of treatment and self-help groups for homosexuals modeled after Alcoholics Anonymous are a resource which the church can support in practical ways.

One practical way a congregation can minister to people struggling with homosexual inclinations is to build up a resource library so that both leaders and lay people are well informed. The books mentioned in the select bibliography are a good start. I would especially recommend the books by Achtemeier, Comiskey, Consiglio, Dallas, Dannemeyer, Foster, Johnson, Magnuson, Moberley, Nocolosi, Payne, Turner, Stafford, van den Aardweg, Wood and Dietrich, and Yamamoto.

Sustaining a ministry of prayer is an important aspect. Of course you will pray for homosexuals and their families, but also pray for those who hate or fear them. Pray that your congregation may have an open, loving attitude based on the *fact* that these are all people for whom Christ died.

You will also want to get in touch with the ex-gay movement. You can get on the mailing list of Exodus International and Homosexuals Anonymous. These groups, also, can use financial support at both the national and local levels. You can make space available for group meetings in your church. You could also work with the ex-gay community to establish a counselling ministry in your congregation.

And finally, you can simply love these people and welcome them into your congregation and your homes.[3] We all have a love deficit in our lives. It is tragic that we all are tempted to turn to sexual perversions to fill this deficit. God has given us the good and beautiful gift of sexual love within marriage. But even that love is not divine. What we need to fill the love deficit in our lives is the love of God Himself. That love we have been given in Jesus Christ and receive through the Holy Spirit. St. Augustine was correct: our hearts are restless until they find their rest in the Lord.

Study Guide Questions

1. Does your church have a double standard where sin is concerned? That is, would some repentant sinners be more welcome than others? Discuss.

2. Why might some churches view slips by ex-gays more severely than slips by ex-alcoholics?

3. Does your church almost appear to condone certain sins? For example, in some churches, slander and contentiousness are viewed as a normal fact of life, although the apostles dealt with them very seriously. What factors might be at work to create such a situation?

4. Can you think of any examples of "corporate sin" in your community? What role have you played in creating or maintaining the situation?

5. "Cheap grace is easy enough to dispense, but it brings no healing." Does your church ever dispense cheap grace? In what situations? What would costly grace involve in these situations?

The fact that the woman is created from the rib of the man is most significant for the author of Gen., ch. 2. The man and woman were originally one flesh, and after the creation of the woman they long to become one again. This reunion is realized in the ecstatic oneness of marital love:

"This is at last is bone of my bones
flesh of my flesh. . . ."

Therefore a man leaves his father and
his mother and cleaves to his wife, and they
become one flesh. (Gen. 2:23-24.)

The author is making the confession of faith that marriage, the body, sexual desire and union, the resulting home and children, are all gifts of a loving Creator and have nothing evil about them. For this reason, the Old Testament celebrates sex (cf. the Song of Songs; Prov. 30:19), the wife "like a fruitful vine," children "like olive shoots around your table" (Ps. 128:3; cf. Ps. 144:12), the sons of one's youth: "Happy is the man who has his quiver full of them!" (Ps. 127:5). There is celebration of life here, in all its fructescence and earthy goodness, an actual reveling and glee in the goodness of the physical. It is as if this author too is joining in that hymnic salute of Gen. 1:31: "And God saw everything that he had made, and behold, it was very good."

Elizabeth Achtemeier, *The Committed Marriage*[1]

CHAPTER EIGHT

Summary and Conclusion

All Christians must constantly struggle with the temptation to be "conformed to this world" rather than "transformed by the renewal of your mind," that we may serve God's will (Rom. 12:2). Nowadays, the assumptions and lifestyle of the liberal middle class are pervasive and attractive to many. The current false gods, one might say, are a "trinity" of sex, money and power.[2] Though sex, money and power are in themselves good, they may all be abused. Indeed, they may even become the idols or dominating reality of a person's life – the ultimate reality, taking the place of God. When sex becomes such a force in a person's life, that person is no longer in the realm of the Christian faith, where sex is seen as a good gift determined by the ends for which God created us. We are in fact dealing with idolatry. Idolatry might seem a strong word, but let's not fall for the simplistic notion that an idol must be a block of wood or stone. It can be an idea or a strong desire. And there are those who recommend idolatry to us in the name of "liberation."

James Nelson has argued that we must move beyond Christian "sexual ethics" into a "sexual theology" which, he claims, ". . . takes seriously the *human sexual experience in our time and place as an arena for God's continuing self-disclosure at the same time that it takes seriously the implications of Christian faith for our sexual lives"*.[3]

To speak of "human sexual experience in our time and place as an arena for God's continuing *self-disclosure*" is nothing less than to claim for sexual experience the status of revelation. In fact, Nelson and some other would-be revisors of Christian ethics[4] argue that Christians should accept adultery, homosexuality, bestiality (Countryman, 1988) and a variety of other "human sexual experiences" as sources of God's self-revelation.

Scripture speaks of God's self-disclosure in the Exodus events and in the life, death and resurrection of Jesus Christ but never in "human sexual experience." As a matter of fact, in ancient times it was the religion of Canaan, of the Baal and Asherah, which linked God's self-disclosure to "human sexual experience." This was a religion that God's people were strictly forbidden to have anything to do with.

The reason for this was clear. As Achtemeier points out,

> . . . there is never any thought in the Bible that sexual intercourse can be revelatory of God, a fact that many contemporary writers on marriage have failed to realize, but a fact that is important for our understanding of sex. The reason for this, moreover, is very clear: Israel was surrounded on every side in the ancient Near East by peoples who practiced fertility rites in their religion. It was thought in those pagan religions, just as it is thought in many religions today, that the life of nature and of man were one, and that by the exercise of cultic prostitution, the fertility of nature could be magically coerced. Human fertility affected the fertility of the gods of nature. Through sex, it was thought, humans participated in the life of the divine. This thought is emphatically rejected by the Old Testament writers (cf. Hos. 2:2-13; Amos 2:7-8; Jer. 2:20-22; 2:23-28; 3:1-5; many other references). There is nothing of God revealed in the sexual act, and

> knowledge of him is not communicated in the mystery of sex. There is no doubt that the sexual life of human beings has a wonder and mystery about it, and the biblical writers acknowledge this mystery, as we have said. They also warn us against calling that mystery "God," just as they warn us against giving God's name to anything in all creation (Ex. 20:4-6; Deut. 5:8-10). The teenagers who think they have discovered something "divine" and beautiful in the backseat of an auto are not only kidding themselves; they are breaking God's commandments and blaspheming his holy name.[5]

In the Christian Scriptures, sexual experience is celebrated as a great gift of God within the marriage relationship, as understood in Genesis. Sexuality is seen as part of God's created order, directed towards procreation and companionship. In both the Old and New Testaments, faithful marriage is seen as the analogy to God's faithfulness to his people and their faithfulness to Him. But neither in the Old nor the New Testament is sexual experience a source of enlightenment *about* God; God speaks through His prophets, through His Son, and through His Holy Spirit. Therefore, in neither the Jewish nor the Christian worldview is there any reason for private sexual experience to be seen as a source of divine revelation, especially not a source that could be in any legitimate conflict with revealed truth.

The simple truth is that homosexual practice is acceptable to people who already accept the sexual ideology current in our society in our time, a sexual ideology that stresses individual choice and "self-fulfilment" as a guide to ethics, usually at the expense of community and commitment, as our current widespread social breakdown shows. It treats the body as a "container" for the "self," in contrast to the Jewish and Christian belief in which, in this world at least, our bodies are part of *who we are.*

Our Christian belief that we cannot make any separation

between our selves and our bodies is one of the reasons that we take sexual morality so seriously.[6]

Those who favour the ideology of our current secular society also favour a contractual model for human relationships, where people contract with each other for the services they desire and simply end contracts which do not seem to be in their interests any more. By contrast, Jewish and Christian belief emphasizes the *covenant*, an agreement that arises out of *the nature of one's being*, and therefore cannot simply be ended if it is deemed to be in conflict with one's current interests. (That was why, for example, God could not simply cast off Israel and choose another people, despite her repeated, appalling lapses into sin. He could not do so because it was contrary to His *nature*.) The Christian belief in marriage as a *covenant* (not a *contract*) explains most Christian groups' unwillingness to sanction divorce, except in extreme cases (and some do not allow it at all).

Ideological commitment to the worldview and belief systems of modern secular society explains the interpretation of Scripture by the homosexual lobby. As we have seen earlier, their commitment leads to efforts to wring meanings out of Scripture which it not only never had but never could have had, all the while ignoring the plain sense with which it speaks.

By identifying themselves as "victims" and "the oppressed", the homosexual lobby has been able to masquerade as a "human rights" or "human liberation" movement in the church. But the following words should alert us to the danger of embracing the homosexual ideology:

> Is the homosexual issue in fact comparable to those other liberation movements of recent decades? At least in one very significant aspect, the answer is No. Quite simply, the Bible explicitly and repeatedly condemns homosexual acts. . . . In this important aspect homosexuality must be viewed differently from other liberation movements.[7]

It is tragic to see the theology of liberation implicit in the

Scriptures discredited by movements that do not have Biblical roots. Harold Wells makes an important point when he writes,

> . . . I would argue that the concern about prior ideological commitment is a valid one, and the moulding of the gospel message to "fit" any predetermined or extrinsic agenda remains open to the charge of idolatry, whether that agenda be the preservation of a status quo or a revolutionary program.[8]

Someone might reply, "Well isn't the union of man and woman in one flesh as the image of humanity an ideology, just like the homosexual ideology?" No, it isn't. The image of the union of man and woman in one flesh as the very type of humanity is not an ideology imposed on Scripture. The image arises *out of* Scripture; it is affirmed throughout Scripture; and it is explicitly and emphatically confirmed by Jesus:

> Jesus answered, "Have you not read that he who made them from the beginning made them male and female?" and said, "For this reason a man shall leave his father and mother, and be joined to his wife, and the two shall become one".[9]

We would all like to sweep the evil spirit of "homophobia" from the household of faith. But those who claim that it can be removed only by the acceptance of the homosexual ideology are really asking us to replace our Christian beliefs from revelation with modern secular ideologies. And these ideologies are evil spirits which would take over the household.

As in the *Rites of Spring*, what appears to be a Dance of Life is in fact a Dance of Death. Is not this attempt to sweep away the old and celebrate the "new", which masquerades as prophetic liberation in the church, merely an invasion by the current thinking of the dominant culture? Historian Modris Eksteins, speaking of the ideology of this century, observed that "the sexual rebel, particularly the homosexual, became a central figure in the imagery of revolt. . . ."[10] Perhaps this aura of glamorous rebellion is the source of the "appearance of beauty and spirituality" that Karl Barth observed to be a lure towards homosexuality.

Christians are tempted to baptize the values of the people to whom they minister. They want to be seen as "open and tolerant." They want to be seen as "loving." And, above all, they want to be "successful" and "listened to" and "approved of". Some think that they can do this by making the Gospel "relevant." From such a point of view it is easy to dispose of the Christian Scriptures as irrelevant and outdated and to proclaim a gospel which is nothing more than one's personal attempt to "catch up with" a popular culture. Or to create a continuum of possible interpretations of specific texts, so as to make their meaning appear uncertain.

The damage this does to the authority of Scripture in regard to sexual ethics is serious in itself. But when this type of Biblical exegesis and interpretation is applied to the whole of Scripture, what is left? It is not only that the central authority and guide for Christian life shifts from the written Word of God to the current opinions of a very self-centred society. It is also that, without the faithful witness of the written Word, how will we hear the living Word? How will we distinguish the Holy Spirit from the spirits of our time? Will we care any more to try?

The Reformation tradition, on the basis of Scripture, tells us that we may trust the guidance of Scripture interpreted in the context of the whole of Scripture. We may trust the Holy Spirit to lead us into truth which is in accordance with Scripture, not in contradiction. When we have very clear guidance, as we do here, we are called to freely, joyfully, and obediently proclaim by word and deed God's will and intention for his beloved world.

Endnotes

Chapter 1: The Homosexual Ideology

1. Karl Barth, *Church Dogmatics* (T & T Clark, 1961) p. 166.

2. Arvid Adell, "Process Thought and the Liberation of Homosexuals", *Christian Century,* January 17, 1979, pp. 46-48.

3. The following outline of the homosexual ideology is from Gary Bullert, "The Homosexual Rights Movement: its ideology, goals and tactics", *Journal of Social, Political and Economic Studies*, vol.12, Spring 1987 pp. 3-27. See too, E. Rueda, *The Homosexual Network: Private Lives and Public Policy* (Adair, 1982).

4. James Greer, Julia Heitman and Harold Lietenberg, *Human Sexuality* (Englewood Cliffs, New Jersey: Prentice Hall, 1984) p. 276.

5. Gerard van den Aardweg, *On the Origins and Treatment of Homosexuality* (Praeger, 1986) p. 9ff.

6. F. J. Kallmann, "Comparative Twin Studies on the Genetic Aspects of Male Homosexuality", *Journal of Nervous and Mental Disease*, 1952, 115, p. 283, 298. An outline of the many faults in this very early study may be found in van den Aardweg, *On the Origins and Treatment of Homosexuality* (Praeger, 1986) p. 14f.

7. See the excellent article by Joe Dallas, "Born Gay?" *Christianity Today*, June 22, 1992, pp. 20-23. Much of the following discussion is based on this article. The unreliable sampling method in the Bailey-Pillard study is common among such studies. The twins were volunteers who responded to advertisements in gay newspapers. Hence you have both the "volunteer error" and unrepresentative samples that distorted the Kinsey Report findings (see p. 25).

8. Ibid.

9. Ibid.

10. Cited in *Toronto Globe and Mail,* Friday, July 16, 1993, pp. A1, A2.

11. Ibid., p.A2.

12. Dallas, op. cit.

13. *Vancouver Sun,* March 13, 1993 article entitled "Lesbianism isn't so much a matter of choice, study says".

14. John Horgan, "Eugenics Revisited", *Scientific American,* June 1993.

15. Ibid., p.124

16. Ibid.

17. Ruth Barnhouse, *Homosexuality: A Symbolic Confusion* (Seabury, 1977) p. 157ff.

18. Arno Karlen, *Sexuality and Homosexuality* (Norton,1971) p. 483, italics mine.

19. Barnhouse, p. 37.

20. Ibid p. 37.

21. Cited in Charles Socarides, *Homosexuality* (Aronson, 1978) p. 34.

22. Allen Bell, "Homosexuality:an overview" in Barnhouse and Holmes, *Male and Female: Christian Approaches to Sexuality* (Seabury,1976) p. 142

23. Judith A. Reisman and Edward W. Eichel, *Kinsey, Sex and Fraud: The Indoctrination of a People*, (Huntington House, 1990) outlines Kinsey's ideology and strategy.

24. Ibid. p. 221.

25. Ibid. pp. 22,23.

26. S.S.Janus and C.L.Janus, *Janus Report on Sexual Behavior*, (John Wiley, 1993).

27. Ibid. pp. 402, 403.

28. Ibid. p. 125.

29. van den Aardweg, *Homosexuality and Hope*, (Servant, 1985) pp. 19, 20.

30. Reisman & Eichel, pp. 194,195.

31. *Commentary*, December 1987, pp. 36-40.

32. Ronald Bayer, Homosexuality and American Psychiatry (Basic Books, 1981) and Barnhouse, *Homosexuality: A Symbolic Confusion* and Charles Socarides, "Homosexuality is not just an Alternative Lifestyle" in *Male and Female*, Barnhouse and Holmes pp. 145-56.

33. Alan Bell and Martin Weinberg, *Homosexualities* (Simon and Schuster, 1978) pp. 308,309.

34. Alan Bell, *Homosexuality: an Overview*, op.cit. p. 139

35. van den Aardweg, *Homosexuality and Hope* op.cit. pp. 59,60.

36. Ibid. p. 60.

37. Bullert, op.cit. pp. 11-14.

38. Church of England, *Homosexual Relationships* (Wickham Press, 1979) p. 16.

39. Richard Knudten, *Crime in a Complex Society* (Dorsey Press, 1970) p. 127.

40. Karla Jay and Allen Young, *The Gay Report* (Summit, 1979) p. 275.

41. Ken MacFarlane and Jill Waterman, *Sexual Abuse of Young Children* (Guildford Press, 1986) p.9.

42. David Finkelhor, *Child Sexual Abuse* (The Free Press, 1984), p. 195.

43. See Barnhouse, Bayer, Hadden, Hatterer, Karlen, Kronemeyer, Moberly, Payne, Schwartz and Masters, Socarides and van den Aardweg, listed in the Select Bibliography.

Chapter 2: What do homosexuals do?

1. A personal conversation cited by Roger J. Magnuson, *Are Gay Rights Right?* (Multnomah, 1990) p. 57.

2. Ibid.

3. William H. Masters, Virginia E. Johnson and Robert C. Kolodny, *Crisis: Heterosexual Behavior in the age of AIDS* (Grove Press, 1988), p. 164.

4. Bernard J. Klamecki, "Medical Perspectives of the Homosexual Issue", in J.I.Yamamoto, *The Crisis of Homosexuality*, (Victor, 1990) pp. 115-130.

5. Institute for the Scientific Investigation of Sexuality (I.S.I.S.) "What Homosexuals Do", (1987).

6. Eugene Rueda, *The Homosexual Network* (Deven-Adair, 1982) p. 37, also T.Quinn, "The Polymicrobial Origin of Intestinal Infections in Homosexual Men", *New England Journal of Medicine*, 309 (1983) 576-582: David Ostrow et al, eds. *Sexually Transmitted Diseases in Homosexual Men*, Plenuar Medical, 1982; L. Corey and K. Holmes, "Sexual Transmission of Hepatitis A in Homosexual Men", *New England Journal of Medicine* 302 (1980) 435-438.

7. Katie Leishman, "AIDS and Syphilis", *The Atlantic Monthly*, January 1988, pp. 20,21; E. Rowe, *Homosexual Politics* (CLA, 1984), p. 17.

8. Buchanan and Muir "Gay Twins and Diseases", *The American Spectator*, Aug. 1984, pp. 17,18; Gerald Mandell et al. eds, *Principles and Practices of Infectious Diseases*, 3rd ed, (John Wiley, 1990), pp. 2280-2284, *British Journal of Venereal Diseases* 53:190, 1977.

9. T. Quinn, op.cit. Ostrow et al., op cit.

10. Randy Shilts, *And the Band Played On: Politics, People and the AIDS Epidemic* (St. Martin's Press, 1987), pp. 18-19. Italics added.

11. William H. Masters, Virginia E. Johnson, Robert C. Kolodny, *Crisis: Heterosexual Behavior in the Age of AIDS* (Grove Press, 1988), p. 164.

12. Ibid. pp. 124, 125.

13. Wm. Dannemeyer, *Shadow in the Land* (Ignatius, 1989), p. 102.

14. Roger J. Magnuson, *Are Gay Rights Right?* (Multnomah, 1990), pp. 40, 41.

15. K. Jay and A. Young, *The Gay Report* (Summit, 1979) p. 281

16. Dennis Altman, *The Homosexualization of America* (Beacon, 1982) p. 9.

17. Dannemyer, op.cit, p. 140.

Chapter 3: Homosexuality and the law

1. D. Altman, p. 9.

2. In *After the Ball*, p. 178, 183. See below for further citation information.

3. For a discussion of the American situation see Roger Magnuson, *Are Gay Rights Right?* (Multnomah, 1990), pp. 67-107. To understand the Canadian sit-

uation you can follow the struggles in Toronto. See the article by Susan Careless in Denyse O'Leary, ed., *A CRISIS of understanding: Homosexuality and the Canadian Church,* (Welch, 1988) and Susan Careless's article "Homosexual proselytization allowed by Toronto Board of Education", *Christian Week,* Aug. 4, 1992, p. 1.

4. Saul H. Fisher, "A Note on Male Homosexuality and the Role of Women in Ancient Greece", in Judd Marmor, ed., *Sexual Inversion* (Basic Books, 1965) pp. 165-172.

5. Lawrence Stone, "Sex in the West", *The New Republic* (July 8, 1985).

6. Letter to Diognetus, 5:1-13, 6:1; edited and translated by Eugene R. Fairweather in *Early Christian Fathers,* volume I of *The Library of Christian Classics,* (SCM Press, 1953).

7. Marshall Kirk and Hunter Madsen, *After the Ball* (Doubleday, 1989), pp. 367-368.

8. William Gairdner, *The War Against the Family* (Stoddart, 1992), p. 357.

9. Ibid. pp. 379-380.

10. see Thomas Geller, *BISEXUALITY: A Reader and Sourcebook* (Times Change Press, 1990).

11. Brian Taylor, ed. *Perspectives on Paedophilia* (Batsford, 1981), p. 121.

12. Ibid. p. XX.

13. Judith Reisman and Edward Eichel, *Kinsey, Sex and Fraud: The Indoctrination of a People* (Huntington House, 1990), p. 216.

14. David Greenberg, *The Construction of Homosexuality* (University of Chicago Press, 1988).

15. Ibid. p. 28.

16. Ibid. p. 487.

17. Reisman and Eichel, op.cit. p. 208.

Chapter 4: What does the Bible say about homosexual practice?

1. Obviously there are unions where only one of these results will occur. But the design of the union is intended to facilitate both.

2. He also affirms celibacy in singleness (Mark 10, 10; Matthew 19, 12).

3. For the best survey of biblical interpretation of these passages see David Atkinson, *Homosexuals in the Christian Fellowship* (Eerdmans, 1979) or Richard Lovelace, *Homosexuality and the Church* (Revell, 1979).

4. American Episcopal Bishop John Spong is a very articulate popularizer of the homosexual ideology. His recent book *Living in Sin*? claims to provide both scientific and biblical arguments for a revision of Christian ethics. While his use of science is equally self-serving, it is his hermeneutic which is most revealing. Even Virginia Mollenkott is "disturbed by his hermeneutics" (*Daughters of Sarah*, May/June 1989, p. 28). New Testament Professor Weaver describes Spong's analysis of the Biblical evidence concerning women as both "strikingly selective and superficial". Spong begins with the observation, "There is no doubt about the fact that the Bible is biased against women". According to Weaver, Spong then buttresses his claim with "a noticeably tendentious survey of the relevant texts, which at times oversimplifies, at times misrepresents, and in no way does justice to the multiplicity and complicity [sic] of the biblical evidence". (Ibid. p. 28). Why is Spong so biased and unfair to the male-female equality trajectory of Scripture? Weaver states that, "The strategy is clear: Spong's evident intention is to build an exegetical case for dismissing 'The sexual morality of the Bible' due to its 'destructive definitions'". (Ibid. p. 29). Weaver declares that this hermeneutical move is unwarranted for two reasons. First, Spong's unconvincing exegesis. Second, ". . . methodologically, Spong has painted himself into a false corner by failing to distinguish between the social realities of the biblical world and the theological vision of the biblical writers". (Ibid.)

5. For example, in his condemnation of the standards of the day, by which men could easily divorce their wives, he reaffirmed the order of creation, drawing from it the principle that a man is not free to simply dispense with a woman he has covenanted himself to.

6. For an excellent outline of the Biblical basis for this theology, see Elsa Tamez, *Bible of the Oppressed* (Orbis, 1982).

7. Lesslie Newbigin, "Response to David M. Stowe", *International Bulletin of Missionary Research*, October, 1988. p. 152.

8. James Nelson, *Embodiment* (Augsburg, 1978), p. 182.

9. The thought is echoed by Paul in I Cor. 7: 3-5.

10. Tom Horner, *Jonathan Loved David: Homosexuality in Biblical Times*, (Westminster, 1978).

11. Robert Wood, "Homosexual Behavior in the Bible", *ONE Institute Quarterly*, vol. 5, no. 1 (1962), pp. 10-19.

12. Laurie Schneider, "Donatello's Bronze David", *The Art Bulletin* 55 (June, 1973).

13. Tom Horner, "The Centurion's Servant", *Insight: A Quarterly of Gay Catholic Opinion*, vol.2 no.3, (Summer,1978), p. 9. And even more amazing, former Jesuit John McNeill in "Gay Theology: Interpreting the Good Book", *The Vancouver Sun,* June 19, 1993, p. C15.

14. R.T. Beckwith, "The Attitude to Homosexual Practices in the Jewish Background to the New Testament" in David Atkinson, *Homosexuals in the Christian Fellowship* (Eerdmans, 1979), p. 97-99.

15. David F. Wright, "Homosexuals or Prostitutes?" *Vigiliae Christianae* 38 (1984), 125-153, also W.L. Peterson in *Vigiliae Christianae* 40 (1986), 187-191 and Wright again in *Vigiliae Christianae* 41 (1987), 396-398.

16. Along with David Wright's article, the following articles raise questions not only about Boswell's exegesis but also about the soundness of his entire argument. See Richard B. Hays, "Relations Natural and Unnatural: A Response to John Boswell's Exegesis of Romans I", *The Journal of Religious Studies* 14 (1986), 184-215 and J. Robert Wright, "Boswell on Homosexuality: A Case Undemonstrated", *Anglican Theological Review*, 66:1 (1984), 74-94.

17. Ibid. p. 201.

18. Ibid. p. 202.

19. David F.Wright, book review of Robin Scroggs, "The New Testament and Homosexuality" in *Scottish Journal of Theology*, 38:1, March 1985, pp. 118-120.

20. Joseph Fletcher in his preface to W. Dwight Oberholtzer, ed., *Is Gay Good? Ethics, Theology and Homosexuality*, (Glide, 1971) p. 8. This notion was expressed in a more subtle way in the United Church of Canada Report which states, "The Bible assumes that everyone is heterosexual", p. 35. And Gerald T. Sheppard describes the Biblical statements concerning homosexuality as "homophobic". See his article "The Use of Scripture within the Christian Ethical Debate Concerning Same-Sex Oriented Persons", *Union Seminary Quarterly Review*, 40:13-35, p. 22.

21. United Church of Canada Report, *Toward a Christian Understanding of Sexual Orientations, Lifestyles and Ministry,* 1987.

22. L. William Countryman, *Dirt, Greed and Sex* (Fortress, 1988), p. 243-244.

23. James B. Nelson, *Embodiment* (Augsburg, 1979), p. 150.

24. Dietrich Bonhoeffer, *Cost of Discipleship* (SCM, 1959).

25. There is at least one study that provides evidence that in his youth Adolf Hitler indulged in homosexual practices. Samuel Igra, *Germany's National Vice*, (Quality, 1945). It is noteworthy that his name does not appear on lists of "famous men" who practised homosexuality. For the real political reasons for Hitler's attack on Röhm and the S.A. see John Bradley, *The Illustrated History of the Third Reich* (Bison Books, 1985), pp. 87-93.

26. Karl Barth, *Church Dogmatics*, III 4 (T&T Clark, 1961) p. 166.

27. Jean Vanier, *Man and Woman He Made Them* (Anglican Book Centre, 1985), p. 66-67.

Chapter 5: All cats are grey: attempts to revise language, theology and ethics

1. See William Gairdner, *The War Against the Family* (Stoddart, 1992), p. 378.

2. Those who want to dig more deeply into this important issue of the Christian language for God are referred to Donald G. Bloesch, *The Battle for the Trinity* (Servant, 1985), John W. Miller, *Biblical Faith and Fathering*, (Paulist, 1989), Alvin F. Kimel ed., *Speaking the Christian God*, (Eerdman's, 1992) and Mary A. Kassian, *The Feminist Gospel*, (Crossway, 1992).

3. Philip Turner, *Sex, Money and Power* (Cowley, 1985), p. 35ff is the basis for the following discussion of the revision of sexual ethics.

4. Malcolm Macourt, "Toward a Theology of Gay Liberation" in Malcolm Macourt, ed. *Theology of Gay Liberation* (SCM Press, 1977).

5. For example, Una Kroll, *Sexual Counselling* (S.P.C.K. 1983).

6. See Jacques Ellul, *Jesus and Marx: From Gospel to Ideology* (Eerdman's: 1988).

7. E. Achtemeier, "The Impossible Possibility: Evaluating The Feminist Approach to Bible and Theology." *Interpretation*, vol. XLII, no. 1, January 1988, pp. 45-57, p. 54. See also Roland M. Frye, "Language for God and Feminist Language", *Interpretation*, vol.XLIII, no.1 January 1989, pp. 45-57.

8. Ibid. p. 55.

9. This translation of the Barmen Declaration, 1934 is from John Leith, ed., *Creeds of the Churches* (Anchor, 1963) p. 517-522.

Chapter 6: Can homosexual orientation be changed?

1. Charles Socarides "Homosexuality is not just an alternative lifestyle" in Barnhouse and Homes, *Male and Female* (Seabury, 1976) pp. 144-155, p. 146, 147.

2. Jean Vanier, *Man and Woman He Made Them* (Anglican Book Centre, 1986) pp. 66-67.

3. See Barnhouse, Bayer, Haddon, Hatterer, Karlen, Kronemeyer, Moberly, Payne, Schwartz and Masters, Socarides and van den Aardweg listed in the Select Bibliography.

4. This section follows van den Aardweg, *Homosexuality and Hope*, p. 39ff. The quotation from Freud is cited p. 141.

5. E. Moberly, *Homosexuality: a New Christian Ethic*, (Attic Press, 1983).

6. There are a number of homosexual self-help organizations:
EXODUS INTERNATIONAL, P.O. Box 2121, San Rafael, CA 94912, (415) 454-1017 is an umbrella organization for the others:
Metanoia Ministries, P.O. Box 33039, Seattle, WA 98133;
Outpost, 734 East Lake Street, Minneapolis, MN 55407 55104;
Regeneration, P.O. Box 10574, Baltimore, MD 21285, and for more information on *Homosexuals Anonymous* (H.A.), modelled on the spiritual steps of A.A., see *H.A. News*, the Official Newsletter of Homosexuals Anonymous Fellowship Services, P.O. Box 7881, Reading, PA 19603, (215) 376-1146 or 1-800-253-3000

Contacts in Canada are:
New Beginnings, P.O.Box 1078, Stn. F, Toronto, ON, M4Y 2T7 (416) 921-6557
Burnaby Christian Counselling Group, 73225 MacPherson Ave., Burnaby, BC, V5J 4N8 (604) 430-1301
Harvest House Homosexual Outreach, P.O.Box 47, R.R. #5, Gloucester, ON, K1G 3N3 (613) 822-1158
H.A. Toronto Chapter, P.O. Box 1078, Stn. F, Toronto, ON, M4Y 2T7. (416) 921-6557
H.A. Barrie Chapter, P.O. Box 1468, Barrie, ON, L4M 5R4 (705) 722-4041
H.A. Calgary Chapter, (403) 262-2627
H.A. Edmonton Chapter, (403) 471-9124
H.A. Red Deer Chapter, (403) 342-0002

Help for Parents and Loved Ones:
Spatula Ministries, P.O. Box 444, La Habra, CA 90631

Help for AIDS Ministry:
Aids Resource Ministries, 12488 Venice Blvd., Los Angeles, CA 90631

7. Two books by "ex-gays" which are especially helpful are Andrew Comiskey's, *Pursuing Sexual Wholeness* (Creation House, 1989) and Joe Dallas's, *Desires in Conflict* (Harvest House, 1991). Both of these books are Biblically, theologically and psychologically sound, as well as expressing deep understanding and respect. A book that can be a life saver for Christian parents is Barbara Johnson's *Where Does a Mother Go to Resign?* (Bethany House, 1979). She is the founder of Spatula Ministries (which is named because of the need to help peel parents off the ceiling when their children declare that they are homosexual). And a very compassionate and helpful book about the AIDS crisis is Glenn Wood and John Dietrich, *The AIDS Epidemic: Balancing Compassion and Justice* (Multnomah, 1990).

8. Barnhouse, *Homosexuality: a Symbolic Confusion*, p. 95ff.

9. Van den Aardweg, *Homosexuality and Hope*, pp. 44, 45.

10. van den Aardweg, *Origins*, p. vi.

11. Ibid.

12. Ibid.

13. Ibid.

14. Ibid.

15. Ibid.

16. Charles Socarides, "Homosexuality is not just an alternative lifestyle", op cit, p. 148,149.

17. Ibid.

18. Charles Socarides in *American Handbook of Psychiatry*, vol.III, 2nd ed. (Basic Books, 1974) p. 296, italics mine.

19. Franz G. Alexander and Sheldon T. Selesnick, *The History of Psychiatry* (Harper and Row, 1966), p. 358 Italics mine.

20. Ruth Tiffany Barnhouse, *Homosexuality: A Symbolic Confusion* (Seabury, 1977), p. 97

21. M. F. Schwartz and W. H. Masters, "The Masters and Johnson Treatment Programs for Dissatisfied Homosexual Men," *American Journal of Psychiatry*, vol. 141 (1984), pp. 173-181.

22. Arno Karlen, *Sexuality and Homosexuality: A New View* (Norton,1971), p. 583.

23. Karlen, Ibid. p. 602.

24. Judd Marmor, "Homosexuality and Sexual Orientation Disturbances", *Normal and Abnormal Human Sexuality* 1519, cited in Denyse O'Leary, ed. *A Crisis of Understanding: Homosexuality and the Canadian Church* (Welch, 1988) p. 128.

25. Karlen, op.cit, p. 569.

26. R. J. Foster, *Money, Sex and Power* (Harper, 1985), pp. 106-112.

27. Ibid. p. 112.

28. Ibid.

Chapter 7: Are homosexuals welcome in the church?

1. Richard Lovelace, *op cit.* p. 94

2. Gowland, William, *Militant and Triumphant* (Nashville: Tidings, 1953).

3. See the very fine article by Stanton L. Jones in the July 19, 1993 edition of *Christianity Today,* pp. 18-25; particularly the concluding section "What are we to do".

Chapter 8: Summary and conclusion

1. Elizabeth Achtemeier, *The Committed Marriage* (Westminster, 1976), p.71.

2. See the two very fine books with very similar titles, Phillip Turner, *Sex, Money and Power* (Cowley, 1985) and Richard J. Foster, *Money, Sex and Power* (Harper, 1985).

3. James Nelson, *Embodiment* (Augsburg, 1979), p. 16. italics mine.

4. These are dealt with in more detail in chapter V, section on ethics.

5. Achtemeier, op cit. pp. 163, 164.

6. See I Cor. 6:15-19, where Paul makes this point.

7. Arvid Adell, "Process Thought and the Liberation of Homosexuals", *Christian Century*, Jan. 17, 1979, pp. 46-48.

8. Harold Wells, "The Question of Ideological Determination In Liberation Theology", *Toronto Journal of Theology* 3/2, 1987, pp. 209-220, p. 212.

9. Mark 10:2-10; Matthew 19:3-9.

10. Modris Eksteins, *Rites of Spring: The Great War and the Birth of the Modern Age* (Lester and Orpen Dennys: 1989) p. 34.

Select Bibliography

ACHTEMEIER, E. "The Impossible Possibility: Evaluating the Feminist Approach to Bible and Theology", *Interpretation,* January, 1988, pp. 45-57.
The Committed Marriage, (Westminster, 1976).

ATKINSON, D. *Homosexuals in the Western Christian Fellowship* (Eerdman's, 1979).

BAILEY, D.S. *Homosexuality and the Western Christian Tradition,* (Longmans, Green, 1955).

BARNHOUSE, R.T. *Homosexuality: A Symbolic Confusion,* (Seabury, 1977).

BARTH, K. *Church Dogmatics, III.1 and III.4,* (T&T Clark,1958,1961).

BAYER, R. *Homosexuality and American Psychiatry,* (Basic Books, 1981).

BELLAH, R.N. *Habits of the Heart: Individualism and* et al. *Commitment in American Life,* (Harper and Row, 1985).

BERGLER, E. *Homosexuality: Disease or Way of Life,* (Hill and Wang, 1957).

BLOESCH, D.G. *The Battle for the Trinity,* (Servant, 1985).

BLOOM, A. *The Closing of the American Mind,* (Simon & Schuster, 1987).

BONHOEFFER, D. *The Cost of Discipleship,* (SCM:1959).

BOSWELL, J. *Christianity, Social Tolerance, and Homosexuality*, (University of Chicago Press, 1980).

BULLERT, G. "The Homosexual Rights Movement: Its Ideology, Goals and Tactics," *Journal of Social, Political and Economic Studies*, vol. 12, Spring 1987, pp. 3-27.

COMISKEY, Andrew *Pursuing Sexual Wholeness*, (Creation House, 1989).

CONSIGLIO, W. *Homosexual No More*, (Victor, 1991).

COUNTRYMAN, L.W. *Dirt, Greed and Sex*, (Fortress, 1988).

DALLAS, Joe *Desires in Conflict*, (Harvest House, 1991).

DANNEMEYER, Wm. *Shadow in the Land: Homosexuality in America*, (Ignatius, 1989).

D'EMILIO, J. and FREEDMAN, E.B. *Intimate Matters: A History of Sexuality in America*, (Harper and Row, 1988).

EKSTEINS, M. *Rites of Spring: The Great War and the Birth of the Modern Age*, (Lester and Orpen Dennys, 1989).

ELLUL, J. *The Subversion of Christianity* (Eerdmans:1986). *Jesus and Marx: From Gospel to Ideology*, (Eerdmans: 1988).

FOSTER, R.J. *Money, Sex and Power*, (Harper, 1985).

FRYE, R. M. "Language for God and Feminist Language", *Interpretation*, vol. XLIII, no.i January, 1989, pp. 45-57.

GAIRDNER, W.D. *The War Against the Family* (Stoddart, 1992).

GORDIS, R. *Love and Sex: A Modern Jewish Perspective* (McGraw-Hill Ryerson, 1978).

GREENBERG, D.F. *The Construction of Homosexuality*, (Univ. of Chicago, 1988).

HADDEN, S. "Treatment of Male Homosexuals in Groups," *The International Journal of Group Psychotherapy*, 16, no.1 January 1, 1966, pp. 13-22. "Homosexuality: Its Questioned Classification," *Psychiatric Annuals*, vol. 6 no.4, April 1976, pp. 38-46.

HANIGAN, J. P. *Homosexuality*, (Paulist, 1988).

HARVEY, J. *The Homosexual Person: New Thinking in Pastoral Care*, (Ignatius, 1987).

HATTERER, L. *Changing Homosexuality in the Male*, (Dell, 1971).

HAYS, R.B. "Relations Natural and Unnatural: A Response to John Boswell's Exegesis of Romans I," *The Journal of Religions Ethics*, 14, 1986, pp. 184-215.

HOUCK, D. A. *Case Study Analysis of Homosexual to Heterosexual Transformation with Overview of the Moberly Model*, (Metanoia Ministries, 1988).

JANUS, S.S. and JANUS, C.L. *Janus Report on Sexual Behavior*, (John Wiley, 1993).

JOHNSON, Barbara *Where Does a Mother Go to Resign?* (Bethany House, 1979).

JONES, Stanton L. "The Loving Opposition", *Christianity Today*, July 19, 1993, pp, 18-25.

KARLEN, A. *Sexuality and Homosexuality: A New View*, (Norton, 1971).

KASSIAN, Mary A. *The Feminist Gospel*, (Crossway, 1992).

KIRK, M.and MADSEN, H. *After the Ball*, (Doubleday, 1989).

KIMEL, A.J. "The Holy Trinity Meets Ashtoreth: A Critique of the Episcopal 'Inclusive' Liturgies," *Anglican Theological Review*, LXXI:1 (1989) pp. 25-47. Editor, *Speaking the Christian God* (Eerdman's, 1992).

KRONEMEYER, R. *Overcoming Homosexuality*, (MacMillan, 1980).

LASCH, C. *The Culture of Narcissism*, (Norton,1978).

LOVELACE, R.F. *Homosexuality and the Church*, (Revell 1979).

MAGNUSON, R.J. *Are Gay Rights Right?* Multanomah, 1990).

MOBERLY, E. *Homosexuality: A New Christian Ethic*, (Attic Press, 1983).

MONEY, J. "Paraphilias: Phenomenology and Classification," *American Journal of Psychotherapy*, 38:2 1984, pp. 164-179.

NELSON, J.B. *Embodiment*, (Augsburg, 1978).

NEWBIGIN, L. *The Other Side of 1984*, (W.C.C., 1983).
Foolishness to the Greeks, (Eerdmans, 1986).
"Response to David M. Stowe," *International Bulletin of Missionary Research*, October 1988.

NICOLOSI, Dr.J. *Reparative Therapy of Male Homosexuality*, (Jason Aaronsen, 1991).

O'LEARY, D. *A Crisis of Understanding: Homosexuality and The Canadian Church*, (Welch, 1988).

PATTISON & PATTISON "Ex-Gays: Religiously Mediated Change in Homosexuals," *American Journal of Psychiatry*, 1980, 137, pp. 1553-1563.

PAYNE, L. *The Broken Image*, (Crossway, 1981).

PIPER, 0. *The Biblical View of Sex and Marriage* (Scribners, 1960).

RINGE, S. *Jesus, Liberation, and the Biblical Jubilee*. (Fortress, 1985).

ROSENBERG, M. "Inventing the Homosexual", *Commentary* Dec. 1987. pp. 36-40.

RUEDA, E.T. *The Homosexual Network: Private Lives and Public Policy*, (Adair, 1982).

SCANZONI, L. and MOLLENKOTT, V.R. *Is The Homosexual My Neighbour?* (Harper and Row, 1989).

SCHWARTZ, M.F. and Masters, W.H. "The Masters and Johnson Treatment Programs for Dissatisfied Homosexual Men," *American Journal of Psychiatry*, 141 1984, pp. 173-181.

SCROGGS, R. *The New Testament and Homosexuality*, (Fortress, 1983).

SHILTS, R. *And the Band Played On: Politics, People and the AIDS Epidemic*, (St. Martin's Press, 1987).

SOCARIDES, C. *Homosexuality*, (Aronson, 1978).
"The Sexual Deviations and the Diagnostic Manual," *American Journal of Psychotherapy*, 32 1978, pp. 414-425.
"Homosexuality is not just an alternative lifestyle," in Barnhouse and Holmes, *Male and Female: Christian Approaches to Sexuality*, (Seabury, 1976) pp. 144-155.

SPONG, J.S. *Living in Sin?* (Harper and Row, 1988).

STACKHOUSE, M. "Thirty-eight Theses on Christian Social Ethics and Sexuality with Particular Reference to Issues Posed by Gay and Lesbian Advocates in Church-related Institutions," *This World*, Spring, 1989, no.25, pp. 119-125.

STAFFORD, Tim *The Sexual Christian*, (Victor Books, 1989).

SWARTLEY, W. M. *Slavery, Sabbath, War and Women*, (Herald Press, 1983).

TAYLOR, B. ed. *Perspectives on Paedophilia*, (Batsford, 1981).

TURNER, P. *Sex, Money and Power*, (Cowley, 1985).
Men and Women, (Cowley, 1989).

VAN DEN AARDWEG, G.
Homosexuality and Hope, (Servant Books, 1985).
On The Origins and Treatment of Homosexuality, (Praeger, 1986).
"Parents of Homosexuals – Not Guilty? Interpretation of Childhood Psychological Data," *American Journal of Psychotherapy*, 38:2 1984, pp. 164-179.

VANIER, Jean *Man and Women He Made Them*, (Anglican Book Centre, 1985).

WILLIAMS, D. *The Bond That Breaks: Will Homosexuality Split the Church*, (BIM, 1978).

WOOD, G.G. and DIETRICH, J.E. *The AIDS Epidemic*, (Multnomah,1990).

WRIGHT, D. F. "Homosexuals or Prostitutes? The meaning of arsenokoitai. (I Cor.6:9. I Tim.1:10)" *Vigiliae Christianae* 38, 1984, pp. 125-153.
"Translating arsenokoitai", *Vigiliae Christianae* 41, 1987, pp. 396-398.
Book review of Robin Scroggs', "The New Testament and Homosexuality" in the *Scottish Journal of Theology* 38:1, March 1985, pp. 118-120

WRIGHT, J. R. "Boswell on Homosexuality: A Case Undemonstrated," *Anglican Theological Review*, 66:1 1984, pp. 74-94.

YAMAMOTO, J.I.ed. *The Crisis of Homosexuality*, (Victor Books, 1990).

About the Author

Dr. Don Faris is the minister at North Lonsdale United Church in North Vancouver, British Columbia. He was ordained by B.C. Conference in 1962. Don served as the assistant minister in a black congregation in Richmond, Virginia in the early 1960s, was a missionary in Zambia, Africa in the late 1960s and has ministered to congregations in B.C. and Saskatchewan. Elected a member of the Saskatchewan Legislature in 1971, Don served two terms, acting as Minister of Education from 1976 to 1978. Out of his concern for alcoholics, Don was asked to chair a Legislative Committee on Liquor Regulations. He was the founding chairman of an alcoholism treatment centre and wrote a Federal/Provincial Training Manual for alcoholism workers. His outspoken critique of government alcoholism policies was described in the *United Church Observer* article, "Canada's Bravest Politician." His Ph.D. from New College, Edinburgh is in the field of Christian Doctrine. Don and his wife Margaret have been active in world development issues for a long period of time. Don's hobbies are walking, reading, table tennis, weight lifting and scuba diving.